D0226864

In Our Dreaming & Singing

In Our Dreaming & Singing
The Story of the
Three Choirs Festival Chorus

compiled by
Barbara Young

Barbara Young.

Logaston Press

LOGASTON PRESS
Little Logaston Woonton Almeley
Herefordshire HR3 6QH

First published by Logaston Press 2000

Copyright text © Barbara Young 2000

All rights reserved. No part of this publication
may be reproduced, stored in a retrieval system,
or transmitted, in any form or by any means,
electronic, mechanical, photocopying, recording
or otherwise, without the prior permission,
in writing of the publisher

ISBN 1 873827 31 8

Set in Times and Lucida by Logaston Press
and printed in Great Britain by
MFP Design & Print, Manchester

To
Friends who are singers and singers who are friends

How great is the pleasure, how sweet the delight
When soft love and music together unite.
Dr. Harrington

But we, with our dreaming and singing,
Ceaseless and sorrowless we!
The glory about us clinging
Of the glorious futures we see,

From 'The Music Makers'
by Arthur O'Shaughnessy

Acknowledgements

Many people have encouraged, helped and provided information leading to the publication of this book and it is difficult to mention them all. However, I am particularly indebted to the following for persuading me to write it down: Percy Arrowsmith, Herbert Baber, Peter Bell, Elizabeth and Rodney Bennet, Anthony Boden, Mary Durrant, Charles Farncombe, Chris & John Harris, Peter Hillier, Tony Jennings, Kevin Kimber, Dr. Roy Massey, Cynthia Morey, Michael Morris, Molly Proctor, Brian Richardson and Dr. Percy Young.

In ferreting out information and illustrations I wish to thank the librarians of Blackburn, Bolton, Bradford, Burnley, King's College Cambridge, Chorley, Gloucester, Halifax, Hereford, Leeds, Norwich, Oldham, Oxford, Preston, Rochdale, Shaw, Wakefield and Worcester, together with staff at The Royal College of Music, Royal Academy of Music, The National Portrait Gallery, and Dulwich Picture Gallery. Specifically, I wish to thank Christopher Guy for the photograph of Worcester Cathedral on the front cover, reproduced by permission of the Dean and Chapter of Worcester; Gloucester Library for permission to use the illustrations on pp.20, 23, 52 and 65; Roy Massey for those on pp.51, 87 and 93; the Trustees of Dulwich Picture Gallery for that on p.*viii*; Gareth Rees-Roberts for those on pp.2 and 111;, Kevin Kimber for both drawing and the use of that on p.43; the *Hereford Times* for that on p.105; and Hereford Cathedral Library for that on p.63 and the British Museum for that on p.28.

I also owe a debt to the Choral Society Secretaries of Birmingham, Bradford, Gloucester, Halifax, Hereford, Huddersfield, Leeds, Wakefield and Worcester for their contributions, and my fellow singers who have offered opinions and encouragement but prefer to remain anonymous. Finally, to Andy Johnson of Logaston Press for his patience and skill.

Contents

		page
	Acknowledgements	*vi*
	Foreword	*ix*
	Introduction	*xi*
1	Opening Service	1
2	Three Choirs	5
3	Singers of the North	11
4	London	17
5	Sarah Harrop	25
6	Invited to Sing	31
7	Just Good Friends	45
8	At a Solemn Music	53
9	Intermezzo	59
10	Choral Conglomerate	69
11	Rehearsal	81
12	Victoriana	85
13	Wind of Change	91
14	On Wings of Song	99
15	Hallelujah	103
	Bibliography	113
	References	114

Gainsborough's portrait of Eliza and Maria Linley,
who sang choruses and solos in the 1770s

Foreword

Much factual information is available concerning the origin of the annual 'meetings of the three choirs of Gloucester, Hereford and Worcester' and the development of these meetings into the internationally renowned Three Choirs Festival of today.

Building upon the first official history of the Festival by the Reverend Daniel Lysons which covered the years to 1812, historians of later generations compiled 'Annals' which understandably focused attention upon composers and their works, conductors, vocal and instrumental soloists, and, since 1724, the amounts raised for the charitable purposes of the Festival. Until the admirable *Official History of the Three Choirs Festival* by Watkins Shaw (1954), followed by *Three Choirs - A History* by Anthony Boden (1992), relatively little attention had been paid to the history of the chorus during the three centuries of the Festival's existence.

To redress that comparative neglect, Barbara Young, herself an experienced and devoted chorus member, has undertaken research to provide answers to many of the questions which she, with intellectual curiosity, had often asked herself about the chorus of which she is proud to be a member.

The questions posed and the answers which she has elicited and shares with us make fascinating reading—not only for fellow performers but also for members of the audience at these historic Festivals.

What of the future? One must assumat that the Festival will continue to prosper in the years ahead and give joy to many generations of music-lovers. In particular one must hope that, throughout the 21st century, the members of the chorus—the backbone of the Festival—will experience exhilaration in meeting the challenges of works yet unwritten, as their predecessors in the 18th century thrilled to the great works of Handel; those in the 19th century to Beethoven and Mendelssohn; and Barbara and her friends in the 20th century to Elgar, Vaughan Williams and Benjamin Britten.

David Willcocks

Sir David Willcocks, CBE, MC
Master of the Choristers and Organist of Worcester Cathedral, 1950-1957

Introduction

The Music in my heart I bore
Long after it was heard no more.
From 'The Solitary Reaper' by William Wordsworth

It was the morning after the night before; the Sunday after the last Saturday evening of the Three Choirs Festival; the day of reckoning; time to come back from that other world and down to earth after a week of concertizing. I was coming home from Gloucester, still on my little pink cloud of absolute happiness, surrounded by an aura of golden joy and still in my other body, the one that thinks it can sing like Felicity Lott or Janet Baker.

My route was over the Malverns, hills of mountainous character if not size, rising out of the mist from the spot at which Gloucestershire, Worcestershire and Herefordshire join and where so much inspiration for music has been found in the air, the colours, the contours, by so many English composers, present and past. I lifted mine eyes unto the hills and thought, that's where I've been, and I really don't want to come down. As one of my friends in the chorus said, "When I'm on that platform, up there singing, Oh, I'm on a pathway to heaven."

The experience of being part of the crew of the Three Choirs Festival is indeed a rare one. It is a privilege to be one of several hundred artisans focusing energy onto producing this week of music; skills and talents collectively creating an atmosphere suitable for the best of human endeavour and aspiration. Minds and muscles equally important in shaping programme and presentation, age and youth equally placed when experience is being handed on to new members of the family—for that is just what we have become from years of singing together. Like all the best families we have things to growl about, pecking orders to work out, care of the elderly and nurturing of the young, and closing of ranks when threatened by new music which we don't understand and strange conductors who don't understand us.

On that Sunday morning in late August, I was suddenly struck with the thought that being a mere grain of sand in this organisation was wonderful in itself, and should be enough, but to be a member of a chorus which had first been convened in Hanoverian times and was still in its full flush of youthful enthusiasm was quite overwhelming. I began to think about the chorus singers of past times. Surely they would have felt the same tingle of anticipation at the start of a concert—did they too want it to begin but never to end?; the same problems over seating on the platform—did they *have* a platform? could they see the conductor?; the same worries over suitable concert-dress—what did those singers of other times have to wear?; the same exhilaration and exhaustion from singing their hearts out, and the same feeling of being on a different planet, removed from normality, away from the responsibilities of everyday life which keep our feet on the ground and our minds sane—did *they* have to abandon home and family while they went off to sing at the Three Choirs Meetings? Nowadays the chorus is collected from the three cities, in a fairly democratic manner and after the obligatory terrifying audition, but it wasn't always the case, so where did they come from and who were they?

Since that morning on the Malverns and as a result of the annual post-Three-Choirs-Festival-struggle-with-reality, I have been much occupied with finding generations of singers who stood where we stand, sang some of what we sing, and whose lives were enriched beyond description and dominated beyond explanation by their having been in the chorus.

I began thinking about my predecessors and assumed their lives would be much like mine until I looked into matters historical and discovered the 18th century ones were 'Ladies from the North', (not 'Queens of the Night', but nearly so). This scrap of information along with 'female singers from Lancashire', culled from the few accounts of past Three Choirs gatherings was so intriguing and so demanding of further investigation that I have spent many a happy hour corresponding with librarians, reading ancient tomes and removing archival dust, in an effort to find out who the 'Ladies' were and why they had to be 'from the North'.

To discover the original chorus girls has been an adventure through three centuries. Since I don't claim to be a historian, my aim has been simply to identify with these people who had the same emotional response to music and the same delight in being with friends of like interests. Through all the literary comments and historical accounts, through quotations and artistic criticisms, through opinion and judgements from the wisest musicologist to somebody coming to the Festival for the first time, one message rings clear. The performer is always servant to the music. He or she has the responsibility of presenting somebody else's creation in the way it was intended to be heard. We are fortunate to have been given that task and it is an honour we respect. The 'Ladies' who set the stage in the 1770s gained their musical knowledge from parents and instructors and in turn passed on their experience to children and grandchildren, so a wealth of inherited wisdom has been accumulated. Maybe that is what we feel in our bones at the beginning of Festival Week.

My particular interest is in the Three Choirs Chorus but I know from experience that all choral singing, starting with the school carol service and the church choir, then Madrigal Group and Choral Society, leaves its mark on all who share the adventure whether in Cardiff, Manchester, Liverpool, London, Gloucester, Hereford or Worcester.

> We are the music makers and we are the dreamers of dreams.
> Wandering by lone sea breakers, and sitting by desolate streams.
> World-losers and world-forsakers, on whom the pale moon gleams:
> Yet we are the movers and shakers of the world for ever, it seems.
> From 'The Music Makers' by Arthur O'Shaughnessy

What follows, therefore, is an account based on a few facts and a lot of circumstantial evidence of the manifestation of the chorus which has been associated with the Three Choirs Festival from the 18th century until the present day, and of the many lives which have been coloured by the gift of musical talent and the opportunity to be part of the Music Meetings at Gloucester, Hereford and Worcester.

The singers come from many walks of life into a family with a great bond of friendship and love within which personality strengths and weakness are of secondary importance. The all-consuming passion is to make music in as beautiful a manner as is humanly possible and to this end The Chorus is, on a good day, enveloped in a harmony of tolerance and communal enthusiasm. The intense emotional thrill derived from a musical performance which rings true as a result of the application and care put into it, is every bit as stimulating as falling in love or eating chocolate but perhaps more difficult to describe; so the intention of this account is to collect and convey an impression of the feelings of previous generations of singers, and of their desire to make glorious sounds. Compare Beethoven's ninth symphony and its performers with Mt. Everest and mountaineers. The symphony is a most uncomfortable piece to sing so why do we want to do it? As with Everest, maybe because it is there; and we, the music makers, need to reach out to touch and be touched by the inspiration that Beethoven offers to us, just as climbers need to be touched by the other-worldliness of the Himalayas.

We all feel a tremendous sense of achievement and satisfaction when things go well, when the spine tingles and the hair stands on end—as it really does sometimes, in a quiet passage from Fauré's Requiem or in the wild excitement of Verdi's interpretation of the same words. On the other hand, there is acute embarrassment when the wrong notes are evident and deep despair and frustration when, for some reason out of the control of the singers the performance lacks conviction, is uninteresting, even dull, and the audience doesn't receive the message that is intended by the composer. The odd wrong note can happen to the best of us, due to a slip up in the pure mechanics of producing the sounds, whether on flute, viola or vocal chords. Much more distressing to the performer is the failure to interpret or transmit the emotional content of music. This is a sin against the art and an insult to the composer. The true musician is constantly aware of his responsibility to listen intently, to feel the power of the music and to give of himself, to subject himself completely to the message inside the sounds. Even the best performer may feel inadequate faced with the immense power of the greatest music. He can rely on technical skill to find the right notes at the right time but there is so much more than time and tune. Music is a form of communication, but the method of writing down the sounds and instructions on how to produce them is only a skeletal signal, a hint at what can be done. Musicians playing or singing together have to be aware of each other, to pull together, to think together. Only then, with the power of communal thought and sheer concentration, can the result lift us out of our ordinariness, off the ground and away into the stratosphere. At that point, often aimed at, and sometimes achieved, the sheer delight of being on the top of Mt.. Everest persuades us that there is a divinity, convinces us that there is a spirituality, something beyond the here and now, to which we mortals must aspire.

> Heart and soul do sing in me.
> Just accord all music makes.
>   From 'Song, to a Spanish tune' by Sidney

1 Opening Service

> We, who with songs beguile your pilgrimage ......
> Who sing to find your hearts, ...
> From 'The Golden Journey to Samarkand' by Flecker

A brilliant fanfare of trumpets, trombones and tubas reaches far into the vaulted ceiling of the cathedral; sounds chase each other up and down the aisle and wrap themselves round every gigantic stone pillar, filling the whole building with clear golden notes and heralding the start of the Festival. Echoes come back and overlap with another cascade of music like waves on the shore line never quite catching up with the previous one before it runs away with the tide.

A dazzling shaft of sunlight cuts through the stained glass windows on the south side of the building, spot-lighting and dappling and dancing on the faces of the people in the nave; the congregation, the audience, the meeting, the gathering; of Right Reverend Lord Bishops, Very Reverend Deans, Right Worshipful Mayors, Honourable Justices of the Peace, the Lieutenant of the County, Upholders of law and order in town and country, Upstanding Clerks of the Courts, who had assembled at the great North Door, prior to filing into their allotted places next to their waiting attendants, and the worthy citizens of the town. All are here in their Sunday very best, a grand and impressive gathering, brightly arrayed with chain of office, mitre, cap and gown, button hole and corsage, carnation and rose, huge hats, fur and silk, lace cravat and cuff, black velvet collar: all here in the heat of an August afternoon, each representing their particular place in the life of the city. Some, no doubt, feel a little foolish in this regalia, others very important. Some, for whom this

The Opening Service at Hereford Three Choirs in 1991,
with Bishop John Oliver seated, centre

experience is new, wonder why they had to join in this pantomime, but self-consciousness can be forgotten as the magnificence of the music takes command. No soul could be unaffected. This is Pomp and Circumstance at its best and indisputably British, so the stiff upper lip and straight back is all part of the show, this great Festival of Music continues as it has done through three centuries.

A shiver of excitement runs from one to another. Up here on the platform, looking down on the assembly, the 200 singers are detached, separated by the distance of one or two pillars and in our capacity as performers, set apart; yet, at the same time we feel a unity with the congregation before us as everyone present in the cathedral becomes swept up in the shared anticipation of the moment. Whilst having our various parts to play in this unique event, we are, of course, all here for the same reason—to share our emotional and intellectual experience with the listener. Each is inter-dependant. An electric charge runs from one to another, from nave to platform and back and we know that we are among the most fortunate of all; highly privileged to belong to and be taking part in this ancient institution.

> Our souls with high music ringing
> O men! it must ever be
> That we dwell, in our dreaming and singing,
> A little apart from ye.
> From 'The Music Makers' by Arthur O'Shaughnessy, set to music by Elgar

The Service begins.

> I was glad when they said unto me we: will go into the house of the Lord.
> Words from the Prayer Book, set as an anthem by Parry

The cathedral resounds with a great mix and blur and muddling up of notes, especially for listeners in the lady chapel, where the sounds have had to bend round and bounce off pillars and walls, and thoughts might dwell on the age of plainsong, when melody was sung without the embellishment of harmony and even without much in the way of rhythmic excitement, but with a simplicity perhaps more suited to the style of architecture.

But this is not Symphony Hall or the Barbican where one goes to hear every note and where the score-reader can follow the music in his own little

The Opening Service at Gloucester Three Choirs in 1998

book. This is the Three Choirs and funny acoustics are not going to get in the way of something unique in history and something important in our lives. These moments have been special to generations of singers from the beginning of the annual Music Meetings somewhere in the first quarter of the 18th century.

2 Three Choirs

Pastime with Good Company.

From a song attributed to Henry VIII

The Three Choirs Festival, or the Music Meeting of the Three Choirs of Gloucester, Worcester & Hereford would seem by definition to belong to the gentlemen and boys of the Cathedral Choirs. But who instigated the Festival, and was it primarily a sacred or secular event?

Music Clubs were very popular in the 18th century, providing a means of entertainment among friends in convivial surroundings, usually the tavern. Certainly the Vicars Choral in Hereford were known to have been particularly active in this field, and without restrictions being imposed on them by deans and chapters as to what sort of music they sang, they met regularly in College Hall and a nearby hostelry, expressly to sing and play rounds and part songs, known in their day as catches and glees. Membership of the Club was not confined to the Cathedral Choir however. As reported by Lysons in the *Annals of the Three Choirs*, published in 1895, 'The Meetings of the Three Choirs of Gloucester, Hereford and Worcester originated in a compact made by members of certain musical clubs of those three cities, to make an annual visit to each other in rotation and continue together two days, for improving themselves in harmony, by the performance of several concerts of music. These clubs consisted chiefly of members of the several choirs, with the addition of a few *amateurs* of music in the several cities and their immediate neighbourhood.' So it seems that right from the earliest meetings, there has been a happy arrangement between clergy and layman to share the making of music.

The adventure of going away for a week of singing; the excitement of meeting up with other musicians and learning from them stories of the musical world; the satisfaction of learning so much music in so short a time, cannot have been so very different in the 18th century from now. But some things have changed. For instance, church music was written for a different balance of voices produced by the ratio of men to boys being about 26 to 10, a situation which existed until financial constraints of early Victorian times considerably reduced the numbers of Vicars Choral—or singing men. This was not a problem in the anthems of the time since they would have been written with these forces in mind, but performances of Handel's oratorios, with their strong operatic flavour, presented an urgent need for more support in the top, or treble line of the choruses.

There is a notice found by Sir Ivor Atkins in the *Worcester Postman* of 14-21 August 1719:

ADVERTISEMENTS.

THE *Members of the yearly Musical Assembly of these Parts are desired to take No-tice, That, by their Subscription in* September *last at* Gloucester, *they are obliged (notwithstanding a false and groundless Report to the contrary) to meet at* Worcester, *on* Monday *the last Day of this instant* August; *in order to publick Performance, on the* Tuesday *and Wednesday following.*

The Meeting referred to as having taken place in 1718 is already an annual event, so there must have been an assembly for some years prior to this date. In fact, Dr. Charles Burney, in his *General History of Music* 1789, writes at length of the state of music in the country in 1720. He lists some of the important events, many artists, performances of operas, concert programmes, all of which are in London except one. This is a reference to September 7th 1720, when 'A sermon is advertized that was preached in the cathedral of Hereford at the anniversary meeting of the Three Choirs of Hereford, Gloster and Worcester.' It was written by Thomas Bisse, 'Chancellor of the said Church'.

Dr. Burney's historical account of the music of the world, the first of its kind, was seen through the eyes of a much travelled musician. It is gratifying to find the Meeting of the Three Choirs mentioned in such a tome, though the fact that Dr. Burney came from neighbouring Shropshire may have made him particularly alert to what was going on in Hereford in 1720. Nevertheless, from its beginning, this gathering of the 'singing men' for special services was obviously an important ecclesiastical, social and musical event in the calendar of the three cathedrals.

6

A RATIONALE *on* Cathedral Worſhip *or* Choir-Service.

A

SERMON

Preach'd in the

Cathedral Church

OF

HEREFORD,

AT THE

Anniverſary Meeting

OF THE

CHOIRS of *Worceſter, Gloceſter,* and *Hereford,* Sept. 7. 1710.

By THO. BISSE, D. D. *and Chancellor of the ſaid Church.*

𝕿𝖍𝖊 𝕾𝖊𝖈𝖔𝖓𝖉 𝕰𝖉𝖎𝖙𝖎𝖔𝖓.

Publiſh'd at the Requeſt of the Audience.

LONDON:
Printed for W. and J INNYS at the *Prince's Arms* at the Weſt-End of St. *Paul's.* 1721.

Notice of a sermon preached by Thomas Bisse

It is possible that the accession to the throne of George I in 1714, with celebrations and much music, or perhaps, a year previously, the signing of the Treaty of Utrecht which concluded the War of the Spanish Succession, could have been an occasion for the three choirs to combine their vocal powers in special cathedral services.

Tempting as it is to keep going backwards looking for a beginning, it is unlikely to be further away than 1713, if only because travel was difficult. Roads were in existence, but used greatly by farm animals on their way to market, by tinkers, carters and waggoners, and in good weather by the wealthy folk in their carriages. All modes of transport involved horses whose heavy feet churned up the mud, but as there was little cottage industry of the sort that called for merchants to go from Worcester or Gloucester to Hereford there really wasn't much communication between the commoners of the three cities. Whatever the date of the first combined choral meetings, they must have been a huge undertaking for all who took part and a commitment which has led to a special relationship between the three counties.

Handel's arrival in England in 1710 proved to be one of those fortuitous events that couldn't have been timed better, and which left an indelible mark on English music. In 1727 he wrote the anthem, Zadok the Priest for George II's coronation and everyone who could, wanted to sing it or hear it. What a way to celebrate faith in the past and hope for the future! We do know that by this time the annual Meeting was well established. Without Handel, England's opera houses and choral societies, organists and orchestras, even royal patronage and inclusion in the European musical scene, would have lacked a particular impetus. Also many a choir would have missed the annual musical treat and uplifting experience of singing one of the greatest pieces of music ever written—Messiah. Maybe choral societies would have evolved anyway, for the British do like to get together for a good sing. Those of us who feel self-conscious and pretend to have no voice when asked to sing solo, find we can unleash vocal chords for the Hallelujah Chorus. Indeed Handel did more for the singers of this country than can ever be measured.

The oratorio, a form in which Handel excelled, appears to have originated in Rome in 1540, when San Philippo Neri founded the Priests of the Oratory. Each week, in the services, the sermon was sandwiched between music-dramas which were acted, spoken, sung and danced, and called oratorios. Much later, in 1720, Handel set Esther, a sacred drama, for the chapel of the Duke of Chandos, at Cannons. There followed a further private performance in 1731, in the house of Mr. Bernard Gates, Master of the Children of His Majesty's Chapel, when the choristers took part with scenery, costume and acting, and another semi-private one by the same singers in the Crown and Anchor Tavern in the Strand. It was then advertised in the *Daily Journal* in 1732 for public performance in York Buildings, Villiers Street, as 'Esther, a sacred drama or ORATORIO', likewise at the King's Theatre, Haymarket as 'a sacred story'. The audience was told beforehand that there would be 'no acting on stage, but the house would be fitted up in a decent manner.' The Bishop of London refused to allow his choristers to appear in a sacred work in costume so they appeared as a standing choir. This then was the beginning of the custom during Lent for theatres to set aside Opera in favour of Oratorio.

Handel took Messiah to Dublin for its first performance in 1742. After that, he concentrated on sacred music, though nothing reached the heights of that one work, which was, from the beginning, to have such an abiding effect on the hearts and minds of the British musician, professional and amateur.

Handel died in 1759, and in 1784, commemoration concerts to celebrate his birth, work and genius were held at Westminster Abbey and at The Pantheon, the fashionable assembly rooms in Oxford Street, London, with five performances of his music. Handel was born in 1685 so the first concerts were a little premature but possibly this was a trial run to make sure that the idea would succeed. If the organisers had any doubts, these would soon have been dispelled by the acclaim with which this gigantic venture was received by the public who flocked to see the spectacle of all the notable musicians of the time and to hear the music performed by 500 voices and instruments. Such was the success of this feast of Handel's music that the concerts became an annual event in London on a scale not previously known in the country. News of their popularity spread across the land to touch parish clerks, church organists and their choirs in many a provincial town, and helped lay the foundations for future choral societies and festivals of choral singing of the sort that other countries do not have.

The anthems of Handel had been firmly established in the Three Choirs Meetings well before this time and his oratorios Samson, in 1748, and Judas Maccabaeus, in 1754, became favourites in the programme, followed in 1757 by Messiah, thereafter performed every year well into the next century.

From the necessity for making a different sound to suit Oratorio performances in the cathedrals of Gloucester, Hereford and Worcester, was born the notion of using an augmented choir. Later this became an entity in itself, the

Festival Chorus, which nowadays carries the responsibility for performing the major choral works of the week. For the last 200 years music has been written for this type of choir, with equal forces in all voices.

In the *Annals of the Three Choirs* and other accounts of the continuance of the event, it is reported in 1771 that 'the only circumstance in which our choirs fall short of those in the Metropolis is lack of balance through want of trebles.' So for this reason, the stewards of the Meetings, those two worthy, and necessarily wealthy gentlemen who, besides taking it upon themselves to underwrite the expenses of the gatherings and hire the performers, were now required to find some extra treble voices to boost the top line. (In the 18th century the two stewards were consistently a member of the clergy and a wealthy landowner.)

The result of this was the arrival, in 1772 of 'Miss Radcliffe and others of the celebrated female chorus singers', as they were called, 'from the North of England'. The fact that they were already known as 'celebrated' implies that these singers were well established performers in London, but the style of writing about the performing artist of the day, whether theatrical or musical, was fairly often expansive and over-blown so it is not possible to know just how celebrated they were! However, they must have had some standing in London for the stewards to have found them at all, and what is without dispute is their ability to sing the soprano line of Handel choruses from oratorio and opera, with a good strong voice.

3 Singers of the North

Hark! hark, the lark at heaven's gate sings.

From 'Cymbeline' by Shakespeare

During the second half of the 18th century the Industrial Revolution was beginning to grip certain parts of Britain. But for generations in Lancashire and Yorkshire there had been a thriving cottage industry, in which wool from the sheep on the moors and fells was spun, woven, dyed and taken for sale in the markets of the large towns. All the work was carried out in the home but workers were used to travelling great distances on foot or by cart in order to sell their produce. Some people from the rural communities would thus have had the chance to mix with town folk on market day and indeed would have become well acquainted with gossip about town life in general and the latest news from London in particular.

Long before the arrival of mechanized weaving, while cloth was still being produced in the home, it is known that the families of spinners and weavers in the Lancashire village of Ellenbrook were teaching themselves to sing, play, copy and compose music to a high standard. Possibly even more highly trained, though still self-taught, was a musical ensemble of Baptists in Dean, a hamlet five miles south-east of Burnley, in the Forest of Rossendale. They were known as the Deign Layerocks (from the Middle English Laverock, a skylark) or Larks of Dean, due to their beautiful singing. One of these weavers invented a device which would, with the aid of strings, pulleys and levers, enable three or four looms to work at the same time, thus leaving him more free time to practise his music making. This was well before the time of James Hargreaves from Blackburn who, in 1764, invented his

11

Spinning Jenny (patented by Arkwright in 1769), a device capable of turning six spindles at once, so that the spinners in the cottages could produce six times the amount of wool or cotton. Unlike the sparse communications along the borders of Wales, those in rural Lancashire were highly developed to accommodate the need for marketing the cotton and woollen products, and, wherever people met, ideas on matters of art and culture would have been bandied about and compared, along with their theories on the improvement of practical skills.

By the middle of the 18th century, many groups of musicians in different parts of the north of England were in the habit of meeting up with each other on a regular basis. These were mostly poor hand-loom weavers with little in the way of formal education. Somehow, some of them managed to learn to read music, perhaps being helped by a musical vicar or his wife. Whatever the beginnings, parts were copied onto the rough paper of the times which was expensive and hard to come by. Quill pens were used and the only form of artificial light was candle. The need for music may not have changed but its availability has. Their commitment to the understanding of the Art cannot be overstated.

The Larks, it appears, wrote their own music, copied and sang the folk tunes of the day and played and sang compositions by established composers, including Handel, reproducing the latter surely in a style far removed from that heard in the house of the Duke of Chandos or the London Theatres, but, nevertheless with great zeal, undoubted enjoyment and real musical acknowledgement of the greatness of that composer.

Not far from the Forest of Rossendale, in the village of Shaw, near Oldham, existed another musical society. This had been established in 1740, with an indenture between nine high ranking members of the community to 'give power and provide funds for the erection of a gallery for the accommodation of the members of the Society at the westerly end of Shaw Chapel.'[1] One of the nine was the Rev. Joshua Stopford, relation of a future organist of both Halifax and Leeds parish churches, and several of the singing members were from the Travis family, a name later associated with many Three Choirs Festivals. In 1766, a Mr. Travis, parish clerk of Shaw, was selling tickets for a performance of Messiah and parts of Judas Maccabaeus at Shaw Chapel. Another family of singers from Shaw Edge were the Nields, whose descendant Jonathan (1769-1843) sang at the Three Choirs as a tenor in 1793 (Gloucester), 1797 (Worcester) and 1800 (Worcester).

September 25th, 1766.

Performance of the "Messiah" Oratorio, with portions of "Judas Maccabeus" at Shaw Chapel, for the benefit of James Newton, organist there.

The instrumental parts by the best hands in this and adjacent counties. Vocal parts by the PRINCIPAL SINGERS of HEY, OLDHAM and SHAW. The Grand Chorus's will be as full as possible, with Drums, Trumpets, etc.

Conducted by Mr. Wainwright.

Doors open at NINE o'clock in the morning, and the performance to begin at Half-past Ten. Tickets to be had at THOMAS TRAVIS, CLERK of SHAW, at the Bull's Head in Oldham, and at Mr. Nield's, Schoolmaster in Rochdale.

Gallery — 1/6d.   The other 1/- each

Notice of the Messiah in Shaw Chapel, 1766

But how had the weavers of rural Lancashire and the West Riding become acquainted with the music of Handel? The world of the working class northerner and that of the gentry in London, for whose entertainment Handel's operas and oratorios were written, were about as far apart as the North Pole and the Equator, yet somehow Handel's music quickly became that of the common folk. Many arias were immediately appealing to the ear and could be learnt by the sons and daughters of the aristocracy and landed gentry throughout the country, since they did indeed have music lessons. For their benefit separate copies of songs and duets (from the operas) were printed and sent off to the major towns. From there they would be copied out over and over again by hand and passed from house to house, from singer to singer; much valued and treasured.

The Larks of Dean and the Shaw Singers were prepared to walk for miles to join other singers and players. Doubtless, on their travels, they would meet up with each other in the tavern and exchange the latest songs. It is amusing to think of an operatic aria being tried out and learnt in the pub. Most music would have been passed on by ear but if their journey to market took them to one of the larger towns they would be able to see the latest sheet music as it arrived from London, quickly commit it to memory or copy it there and then and take it back home, a prize to be savoured like the poacher's rabbit. The finished result might well have been, like the end of Chinese Whispers, a modified version of the original, and without doubt, the performance of the piece, with home-made instruments and a style of singing more often associated with folk song than theatre performance would have been far removed from that heard on the London stage, and in surroundings very foreign to that patronized by royalty. The fact remains, however, that during the second half of the 18th century, in working class rural Lancashire and Yorkshire there were amateur musicians enjoying the complexities of Handel's music as an extension to their daily fare of hymn tunes and folk ballads, while the delights of such music were still on the distant horizon for the majority of the provincial population of Britain. William Mason, canon and precentor of York Minster wrote later in his *Essays on English Church Music*:

> '... since the rage for Oratorios has spread from the capital to every Market town in the Kingdom, country musicians can by no means be satisfied unless they introduce chaunts, Services, and Anthems, into their Parish Churches, and accompany them with scolding Fiddles, squalling Hautboys, false-stopped Violoncellos, buzzing Bassoons; all ill-tuned and worse played upon, in place of an Organ, which, if they had one, they would probably wish to improve by such instrumental assistance.'

Gradually, roads were improved, vehicle traffic became more efficient and the journey to London, which in 1757 had taken four days, could, in favourable conditions, be reduced to two days by 1770. With the possibility of greater contact, northerners were quick to imitate the better aspects of London high-life, while filtering out some of the sillier and more expensive excesses. Thus, Leeds in the 18th century developed as a social centre with a lively interest in the arts, patronized largely by wealthy cloth merchants, who were only too pleased to pay for the erection of new public buildings as solid indications of their generosity to the city.

Hand in hand with this materialism was the sincere wish to promote science, art, drama, literature and music 'to the improvement of the human

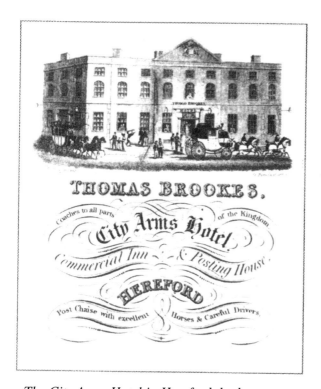

THOMAS BROOKES,

Coaches to all parts *City Arms Hotel* of the Kingdom

Commercial Inn — & Posting House

HEREFORD

Post Chaise with excellent Horses & Careful Drivers.

The City Arms Hotel in Hereford, had grown to become one of the city's main coaching inns in the 1830s to 1850s, with services to London, Birmingham and Liverpool, as well as south-west and central Wales

mind and spirit'.[2] The overwhelming desire of most workers in Leeds or any other industrial town at this time was to elevate themselves to a higher 'class' and one way to do this was by becoming cultured. So the wealthier families became the Nouveau Riche, who promoted concerts and set up schools, and the less wealthy, though ambitious, upper working or lower middle class citizens could benefit from the entertainment, education and status value on offer.

Back in London, from 1750 the city was the scene of enormous artistic activity in all directions. Music, painting and drama were in abundance; Georgian Architecture, still greatly admired and copied today for its clean lines and geometrical style, was being planned by Richard Nash in London and John Wood in Bath; Thomas Sheraton was designing furniture; Thomas Gainsborough was portraying the families of the nobility; David Garrick, born in Hereford, was manager of Drury Lane Theatre.

This blossoming cultural activity led to a search for actors and singers, and some of the girls from the north would have been spotted by theatre impresarios. Tate Wilkinson, who built up a theatre circuit in Yorkshire in the late 18th century, was in touch with Drury Lane and Covent Garden theatres in

London, so his company were able to transfer to the London stage with some knowledge of what to expect. Even if these girls were not acquainted with the acting profession at first hand, they would have followed the fortunes of others who were, and, since there were relatively few big names in the world of music and drama compared with later times, their arrivals and departures, love-affairs, physical appearance, artistic successes and failures, coughs and colds, and temper tantrums would have been the subject of much discussion in drawing room and tavern, in concert hall and boarding house.

4 London

The city is built to music, therefore never built at all
and therefore built for ever.

From 'Guinevere' by Tennyson

The first advertised public musical entertainments in London appear to have been given in the theatres, which, from at least 1602, were accustomed to provide a programme of music before the play began. But the idea of a specific musical performance without the play, open to the general public with payment at the door, came from John Bannister, a violinist, who offered his house in Whitefriars for that purpose in 1672. 'He gathered around him a little body of performers and gave a programme daily at four.' These concerts continued for six years and were extremely popular as 'he found means to procure the best hands in towne and some voices to come and performe there, and there wanted no variety of humour.'.[1] One concert is advertised as 'A Parley of Instruments'.

Mr. Bannister was followed in 1678 by Mr. Britton, a coal-merchant and a self-taught musician and scholar who had a loft over his coal house which he converted and used for 36 years as a music room. It contained a tiny organ on which Handel played soon after his arrival in England. Mr. Britton charged ten shillings a year and supplied coffee at one penny per cup. He could count among his friends some of the most cultured people of his time and many of the nobility.

Next to take on the mantle was Mr. Hickford, a dancing-master, in St. James Street, Piccadilly, who, in 1714, having rooms of considerable size for his school, was able to offer premises to many visiting foreign singers and players for their 'benefit concerts' and as rehearsal rooms. From then on, there was an enormous increase of public concert giving, greatly patronized by Royalty which helped to spread its popularity, and there emerged a new style of building, the Music Hall or Music Room designed to accommodate an audience that would sit still and listen in respectful silence. This name is not to be confused with the Victorian 'Music Hall', a later development from tavern events of organised entertainment with a master of ceremonies, ale, merriment and audience participation.

Operatic productions had preceded instrumental concerts. In 1656, 16 years before John Bannister's concerts began, an Opera House was opened in Covent Garden. This was at the time when entertainment through the spoken word was forbidden by the Puritans, whilst singing *was* allowed. The effect was to make music more available to the common man, and engender a feeling that the musician was a slightly more respectable creature than the actor.

For nearly 40 years after his arrival in 1710, Handel was the key figure at the Opera House in the organisation of musical life in the capital and beyond. He seems to have had a gift for dealing with the business side of running theatres and opera houses as well as providing the music. It was an added stroke of luck that the Hanoverian monarchs enjoyed going to the opera and to the theatre. Indeed all the world and his mistress could attend the play, from the lowest level of society to the king, and many a liaison was made—and broken—between Duke and servant girl, and between Prince and actress in the heady atmosphere of Covent Garden and Drury Lane.

In the mid-18th century only two theatres had a Royal licence to perform plays. As more were permitted, so, more were re-named 'Royal' or 'His Majesty's' or 'King's Theatre'. But to get round the limited opportunities to present drama, an entertainment would be billed as 'A Concert of Music with Public rehearsal of a Play', although usually the play was as complete in its production as the musical items. At Drury Lane theatre in 1732, Dr. Charles Burney noted that 'There was no concert now without a solo, nor play without a concerto.'

To be a success on the stage, one was required to be a musical actor or a dramatic musician. Many young singers, particularly ladies who were worshipped for their beauty as much as for their musicianship, later took to the stage as actors and actresses. One such was Miss Arne, sister of Thomas—later Dr.—who first appeared on the stage as a singer in 1732 and subsequently became a tragic actress. Thomas Arne's oratorio, Judith, (1761) is remarkable for the fact that in its production women singers appeared for the

Glocester Music-Meeting.

THE MEETING of the THREE CHOIRS of GLOCESTER, WORCESTER, and HEREFORD, will be held this present Year at GLOCESTER, on Tuesday the 9th of September next, and the three following Days.

On Wednesday Morning, at the Cathedral Church, PURCEL's TE DEUM as altered by Dr. BOYCE, a JUBILATE by PERGOLESI and other Masters; an ANTHEM composed by Dr. BOYCE suitable to the Occasion; a PSALM by Dr. STEPHENS with instrumental Accompaniments, and the celebrated CORONATION ANTHEM of Mr. HANDEL's. In the Evening, at the Boothall, the Oratorio of JUDITH.

On Thursday Morning, HANDEL's GRAND TE DEUM and JUBILATE, an ANTHEM by Dr. STEPHENS, and the CORONATION ANTHEM repeated. In the Evening, at the Boothall, the celebrated Pastoral of DAPHNIS and AMARYLLIS, the Music by HANDEL, PERGOLESI, JOMELLI, &c. &c. And

On Friday Evening, at the Boothall, the MESSIAH, or SACRED ORATORIO

There will be a grand Band of Vocal and Instrumental Performers from London, Oxford, Salisbury, Bath, and the adjacent Choirs.

The principal instrumental Performers Signor Pinto, Signor Soderini, Signor Storacci, Mr. Simpson, Mr. Miller, Mr. Adcock, Mr. Richards, Mr. Jackson, Mr. Tewkesbury, Mr. Lates, &c. &c.

The principal Voices, Miss Brent, Mr. Norris, Mr. Corfe, Mr. Price, Mr. Matthews, Master Parry, &c. &c.

The Band to be led by Signor PINTO; and the Music conducted by Dr. STEPHENS.

    THOMAS TRACY, Esq; and
    The Rev. F. TRACY TRAVELL, } Stewards.

N. B. Each Morning, after Service at the Cathedral, there will be a Collection made for the Benefit of Clergymen's Widows and Orphans.

Notice in the Gloucester Citizen *in 1766 advertising the Music Meeting to include Judith by Arne*

19

first time in the chorus. Judith was performed at the Gloucester Music Meeting in 1766 in the evening concert at the Boothall. There is no record of how the chorus was assembled, nor who they were, but it may be the first time that a ready made band of singers was taken to the Music Meeting of the Three Choirs, and conjecture suggests that the musicians who learnt their parts in the London performances at Drury Lane could have travelled to Gloucester to

Cartoon showing a performance of Judith
(source unknown)

repeat their success. Compared with later times there were very few singers around anyway, and these would have taken the solo parts as well as singing in the choruses.

Opera also formed a link between drama and music, combining the skills of acting and singing, and allowing performers a passage from one art form to the other. Handel, coming to England via Italy where opera was rampant, arrived with a good working knowledge of how to write and present it in the Italian mode. He kept in touch with many Italian musicians, instrumentalists and singers, whose style of performance and voice production became fashionable, much sought after, and something to be imported by the best theatres. He travelled regularly to the continent to find the best vocalists for his operas, writing especially for particular voices. Italian singers who came to London were idolized for their stage manners and imitated in their vocal style, although—or perhaps because, it was very much more elaborate than that to which audiences here had previously been accustomed.

But opera was to lose ground in the popularity stakes, partly, perversely, because of the continual importation of singers from Italy. The English loved lady soloists because they were pleasing to look at, but found the concept of the Italian castrati soprano or contralto more difficult to cope with. The contrived tone did not have the same appeal as the natural female voice. Another reason for the decline in popularity of Italian-style opera may well have been the expense of production when a soloist was able to command a fee of several hundred pounds, a truly astronomical sum for those times. But possibly, the novelty value of this foreign spectacle just wore a little thin. It was time for a change and public taste in music shifted to something outwardly more restrained and decorous. Oratorio began to assert itself in the hearts and minds of patrons and musicians alike.

At the same time a counter-balance to the almost sycophantic leaning towards anything Italian, had come from the poet Gay and his collaborator Dr. Pepusch, who between them arranged a collection of 18th century popular songs to form The Beggar's Opera. This parody pokes sly fun at the fashionable opera of the period. First produced at Lincoln's Inn Fields Theatre in 1728, its success and that of the many imitations that followed, was a serious blow to the Italian Opera in London, of which Handel was then, and for many more years the leading exponent. It was intended as a political satire, hitting out at the sense of corruption surrounding the Prime Minister, Hugh Walpole and his satellites. A sequel called Polly was forbidden by the Lord Chamberlain and not staged until 1777.

The Oxford Companion to Music, mentioning the Beggar's Opera, states:

'... Newgate was the chief prison in London for criminals awaiting trial and some of the scenes of the opera are placed in it. The age was one of callous indifference to poverty and suffering, when men, women and children were transported or hanged for trifling offences without the prevalence of crime being checked thereby. In the pages of this opera and the pictures of the contemporary, Hogarth, 1697-1764, one sees a vivid representation of the reckless, dissolute and predatory spirit of a large section of the city population of England before the works of the Wesley family, Whitfield, Howard and other social and religious reformers.'

A visitor to London in the late 18th century would have been struck by the widening gulf between rich and poor. The king and his court spent lavishly on the arts, providing some employment within the world of theatre and music, but the lowest classes were in dire straits and it was left to the social reformers of the day to stir the city's conscience into action. 'Milk [was] carried through the streets in open pails, exposed to foul rinsings discharged from doors and windows, spittle, snot and tobacco quids from foot passengers, overflowings from mud-carts, spatterings from coach wheels, dirt and trash chucked into it by roguish boys for the joke's sake ...' So wrote Tobias Smollett in *Humphrey Clinker* in 1771. Sanitation was still a thing of the future.

The Enraged Musician by Hogarth c.1737
Prospero Castrucci, a violinist in the Covent Garden Theatre, is seen
fighting a loosing battle with his patience as he tries to study the score of
the Beggar's Opera. This gentleman was well known for his volatile temper

Mary Linley (see also frontispiece)

The Oratorios thrive abundantly - for my part, they give one an idea of heaven where everybody is to sing, whether they have voices or not.

Horace Walpole, on hearing Judas Maccabaeus in 1747

After Handel's death, the Lenten Oratorios, whose function it was to fill up the days of the week when operas would normally be performed, were continued by J.C. Smith, Handel's amanuensis. John Stanley, the brilliant blind organist for whom a new organ was expressly built in Drury Lane Theatre is said to have had a memory so retentive that he could accompany an oratorio after one hearing—so the money for the new organ was well spent! After him came Thomas Linley, an organist from Bath, whose son-in-law, Richard Sheridan, had just become manager of Drury Lane.

Linley's daughters, Elizabeth (1754-1792) and Mary (1763-1784), were both singers of repute, in fact, Elizabeth was portrayed in a play by Samuel Foote, as The Maid of Bath in which her virtue, beauty and innocence are extolled at great length. Her voice was described as 'angelic, soft, sweet, and affecting' and her physical presence as 'perfection'. She was singing in public in concerts promoted by her father in Bath at the age of 12, and a year later appeared at Covent Garden. By 1770, aged 16, she was famous throughout the country and sang at the Worcester Music Meeting of that year as a soloist, to be joined the following year by her younger sister, who may not have sung the solo items then, being only eight years old! Nevertheless she certainly did so in subsequent years at Hereford and Gloucester. One marvels at the youth and talent of these two girls, tackling music of great complexity, and wooing an audience with their voices. Their singing lives were short, however. In 1773 Elizabeth eloped with, and later married Sheridan, who did not wish her to continue appearing in public, though having been invited to sing at Hereford in 1774 she honoured that agreement, giving her fee to the charity which supports the widows and orphans of the three dioceses. Mary sang at the Meetings until 1776.

Into this world came the girls from the north. Coming from an environment which was still rural, although busy with domestic industry, they were plunged into a whirlpool, a kaleidoscope, a world of vast contrasts between rich and poor; with a great divide between gentleman and pauper and a clearly defined line between master and servant, between patron and artist.

5 Sarah Harrop

An admirable musician! O she will sing the savageness out of a bear.

From 'Othello' by Shakespeare

Back in northern England, music was flourishing on several fronts. An organ had been installed in Leeds parish church in 1713 and William Crompton was appointed as organist a year later. Besides the dances held in the Assembly Rooms during the winter months, there were occasional concerts, including some given in 1741 by Mr. John Parry, the blind harpist from Wales, a great friend of Handel, David Garrick and Joshua Reynolds, and house musician to Sir Watkin Williams Wynne, one of many associates of the Earl of Sandwich whose name crops up again and again in music-making circles. With the appointment of Mr. Crompton it became the responsibility of the church organist to co-ordinate and direct concerts in the Assembly Rooms. By 1760 music was being played in churches for enter-tainment besides for worship. In 1767 singers from Holbeck Chapel, Leeds, on the south side of the River Aire, celebrated the anniversary of King George III's succession with Purcell's Te Deum and Grand Coronation Chorus, a rendering which was such a musical success that at Christmas that year they sang appropriate parts of Handel's Messiah. This must have been one of the Monumental Moments in the history of Leeds' choral singers as in the following year parts of Messiah were performed in the Assembly Rooms no fewer than 18 times. The *Leeds Intelligencer* records the 'delight and satisfaction of the audience', but it is only possible to speculate on the impact that this music would have had on any local singers recruited to augment 'the company of most eminent performers from various Parts of

England', knowing that, a few years later in 1772, some of them would be required to 'assist the treble line' of the Choir in the Gloucester Music Meeting.

Somewhere in all these new activities there was a chance for young girls to be taught the techniques of singing. It is more than likely to have been in chapel under the guidance of an enlightened minister or organist. The new Methodist Chapels were places where enthusiastic singing was encouraged, and indeed, John Wesley, co-founder of Methodism with his brother Charles, published a pamphlet in 1770 titled *The Grounds of Vocal Music*, giving theoretical instruction and seven 'Lessons for exercising the Voice'. As far as is known, hymns were sung in unison in chapel but the interest in and awareness of harmony and part-singing was triggered by the daily arrival of new songs, ballads and dances from London and particularly by the music of Handel which was now available to anybody who could obtain copies from the several music shops that opened in Leeds. The new fashion soon led to notices such as that quoted here:

Instruction in the Art of Singing
for those who wish to avail themselves
will be offered
at
THE ASSEMBLY ROOMS
KIRKGATE
LEEDS

Yet, a year earlier than the Leeds' concerts just mentioned, in August 1766, according to the *Leeds Intelligencer* there appear advertisements and a subsequent report on the opening of the new organ at Halifax parish church with a performance of Messiah. What seems certain is that parts of Messiah had now become the staple diet of singers and were performed in Liverpool, York, Halifax and Leicester by the same peripatetic band of musicians. These singers were brought together by Joah Bates under the instruction of the Earl of Sandwich who paid for their travel and board. It seems likely that the Bass, Tenor and Alto parts were taken by gentlemen of the church or cathedral choirs but since the number of boys used then was considerably less than now,

At the Opening of the

N E W   O R G A N,

In the PARISH-CHURCH of *Halifax, Yorkshire*,
On Thursday and Friday the 28th and 20th of this instant August,
Will be performed, with the Affistance of a very numerous Band of the
moft eminent Performers both Vocal and Inftrumental, from
various Parts of England,

The   M E S S I A H,

An ORATORIO, compofed by Mr. HANDEL.
Between the firft and fecond Acts,

A CONCERTO on the ORGAN.

TICKETS to be had at the White-Lion, the White-Swan, the Talbot
and of Mr. Bates near the Church, at 5s. and 2s. 6d. each.
The Doors to be opened at Nine o'Clock in the Morning each Day,
the Performance to begin at Half an Hour after Ten.
There will be an Affembly each Evening at the Talbot.
N. B.   An ORGANIST is wanted.   Any Perfon who is inclined to
offer himfelf a Candidate, may apply for farther Particulars, to the
Rev. Mr. Bates at Halifax.

Notice in the Leeds Intelligencer *1766 announcing the Messiah in Halifax*

more strong voices were needed to support the long taxing choruses, and the local girls soon learnt the treble line to perfection.

The career of one of these girls is known to us. She was Sarah Harrop, born in 1755 into a poor but industrious family of spinners and weavers in Saddleworth. She showed great vocal ability and her parents gave her such musical training as was available and determined by their means. For lessons in general musicianship as well as singing, Sarah was sent to Mr. Stopford, organist at Halifax from 1766 until 1819.

A very strong tradition of choral singing, already begun by the weavers and spinners, was now taking over the recreational life of Halifax, so that Charles Dibden, in his account of a 'Musical Tour' writes of the town thus: 'Children lisp "For unto us a Child is Born", and clothmakers, as they sweat under their loads on the Piece Hall, roar out "For His yoke is easy and His burthen light". More than one man in Halifax can take any part in the chorus of Messiah, and go regularly through the whole oratorio by heart.'

Mrs. Sarah Bates
(née Harrop) in 1797

Parts of Messiah were performed regularly at the parish church from 1766 onwards. Sarah would have heard these when a very young girl, or been one of the performers when, aged 11 or 12, her voice became a great asset to the choir.

At the time when the teenage Sarah's singing voice was being discovered and nurtured by the organist, there was a young man called Joah Bates in the town. His father, a keen amateur musician who held a choral club at his own home, was the parish clerk, a position which gave him considerable authority in the cultural and political activities of the district. Joah was educated at the Free Grammar School and went to Cambridge where he became a Fellow of King's College and proceeded to gain an M.A. While there, he involved himself in the musical life of the university and cultivated the friendship of numerous aristocratic music lovers, notably the Earl of Sandwich, Dr. Howard and Sir Watkin Williams Wynne. Later, Joah took employment as secretary to the Earl of Sandwich and later became a commissioner in the Victualling Office. Here he was able to add to his numerous wealthy and influential contacts, at the same time maintaining a fervent interest in music making, which much later, led him to being the organiser of and a performer in the Handel Centenary Celebrations of 1784.

Whilst furthering his career, this young man came back to Halifax with copies of Messiah which he directed in the parish church in 1766. He probably first met Sarah at the concerts. She would have been only 11 years old but could well have been singing in the choruses, joining the colleagues whom Joah had brought from London and Cambridge. He was soon captivated by her voice and personality, and their lives grew ever closer on the concert platform.

Through the encouragement of both Joah and Mr. Stopford, Sarah was given the opportunity to sing in counties outside her own and this soon led to her also being heard by Dr. Howard. He is said to have exclaimed on the spot 'that the female he had just heard would one day throw all the English, nay even the Italian, female singers far behind her; for he had never before heard such a natural delicacy of taste, and such surprising musical excellence in any Englishwoman, and in but very few foreigners.'

Dr. Samuel Howard, 1710-1782, had been a chorister at the Chapel Royal, an organist and a composer of music for pantomimes at Drury Lane Theatre. He met Joah Bates when they were both studying at Cambridge and graduated as a Doctor of Music in 1769. It was while on a talent-spotting exercise to find singers for performances of Messiah that he heard Sarah's voice.

Thereafter he became partly responsible for conveying Sarah, Miss Radcliffe and others from the North of England down to London, to sing in the oratorios at Drury Lane and Covent Garden and on to the Three Choirs Meeting. He was an associate of leading actors and musicians of his time and also of Lord Fitzwilliam, Lord Exeter, and other influential amateurs whose names keep cropping up in histories of music and whose wealth and power was used to great advantage in supporting the Arts. Howard's anthem was sung at the Worcester Three Choirs in 1776 and the Gloucester Three Choirs of 1778. At Sadler's Wells Theatre in 1779 he contributed airs to a masque called 'All alive in Jersey', or 'A Fig for the French', along with those of Thomas and Michael Arne and others.

Through Dr. Howard, Sarah and Joah found themselves both involved in the music scene in London under the patronage of the Earl of Sandwich and his friends who met regularly in London at an all male club devoted to the performance, by the members of the club, of the latest glees, rounds and catches. But the Earl of Sandwich had fingers in many pies and could provide male or female performers for any type of musical production. In 1776 this same group of enterprising amateurs extended their energies into forming The Concerts of Ancient Music, whose purpose was the promotion of music written more than 20 years previously. That of Handel came well within the rules so his oratorios received well-earned attention.

Joah was appointed conductor of these concerts. Sarah widened her repertoire sufficiently to appear within a few years as a principal or solo singer and at Gloucester in 1778 was able to command a fee of 100 guineas. They married in 1780, three years after her London debut in Judas Maccabaeus at

On Monday the 29th of June we went to Cambridge where we met Joah and Miss Harrop. I take it for granted that you have heard of Miss Harrop's being engaged to sing at the Oratorios in Cambridge. The two or three days before the Musical Celebrity began we were much engaged in College Rooms, walking over the University and to Pot Fair which at that time was very fashionable. On Thursday 2nd of July there was prayers and a sermon at St Mary's Church and in the course of the Service the Jubilate Te Deum and Coronation Anthem was performed and in the evening 'Alexander's Feast' in the Senate House. On Friday morning (3rd) at Church 'Judas Maccabeus' and in the evening at the Senate House a Grand Miscellaneous Concert. ... On Friday morning Lord Exeter came to Cambridge on purpose to take your brothers and Miss Harrop back with him to Burghley, as soon as he understood that I was at Cambridge he came to our lodgings on purpose to give me an invitation to be one of the party, which you may be sure I did not decline. On Saturday morning at Twelve his Lordship came in his coach to our lodgings and took up Mrs. Bates, Miss Harrop and myself, Joah and a Mr. Hey went in a post chaise, and the honourable Mrs. Walsingham and her three daughters in their own chariot. ...

Letter from Mr. Henry Bates to his daughter, July 1778

Covent Garden where she came to be much in demand as a Handelian Oratorio singer. Here lies a link with the goings-on in Hereford, Gloucester and Worcester, for the stewards of each Music Meeting had, as one of their tasks during the preceding months, to travel to London in order to hire the instrumentalists and the choral and solo singers. What more reliable source could they go to than that provided by Messrs. Bates, Howard, Sandwich and Wynne, from where, in 1772, they hired a group of six female singers. These were Sarah Harrop, Miss Radcliffe and four others, selected from a larger number brought to London from towns and villages on the borders of Lancashire and Yorkshire.

6 Invited to Sing

A North-country maid up to London had strayed
Although with her nature it did not agree.
She sang and she sighed, oh so bitterly she cried
How I wish once again in the north I could be.
Oh the oak and the ash and the bonny ivy tree
How they flourish at home in my own country.

Traditional folk song, *c*.1650

The following letters are reconstructed from fragments left by Ellen and other north country girls from about 1770 onwards. They shed light on the social background of some of these girls so that the enormous adventure which they undertook when they left home to enter the world of music and drama can be appreciated; a world created by musicians, actors, and the aristocracy. They would be subject to the demands of royalty and the whims of the gentry, and dependent upon the taste of the impresarios of the day whose task it was to hire or fire them.

Dear Mother,
This letter is to let you know that I have, at last, arrived safely in London. The journey was so long that I had begun to think we should never see the end of it; and I often thought longingly of home and my dear brothers and sisters. We were two days in the coach all told, although there were stops at the inns when the

horses had to be changed, and the passengers were able to alight in order to stretch their cramped legs and breathe some clean air after the stuffiness of the coach. Dr. Howard looked after our party in the way of paying for the food and drink and finding rooms in Leicester for us to spend the night. These were clean and dry but Fanny was coughing a lot instead of sleeping because of the fact that smoke was coming through from the fire in the room below. I was worried that she might have caught a cold, and then what would she do when it came to the time to sing? She was well the next day, however, so we were able to continue on our way. It would not be good to have to travel with a sickness as the coach bumps and rattles a great deal and the windows have to be kept closed to keep out the dust. The air inside the coach becomes quite foul after a few miles, but the passengers who travel outside on the roof are worse off. They are so cold that their whole body is numb when the next stop is reached and they have to be helped down and into the warmth of the Inn. ...

London, 1771

... Already I feel as if we have gone to a strange country. Everything here is so different from home. London is so big. The streets seem to stretch on for ever and ever. I do miss the moors and the green of the grass, though we can walk along the side of the river and see the view, and the great bridge at Blackfriars. This year we have lodgings in Covent Garden. Dr. Howard found them for us as he knows a great number of actors and actresses and says they all live in this part of town. There are two theatres near to our rooming house. One is the Theatre Royal in Covent Garden, the other is in Drury Lane.

Mrs. Bennet, our landlady is very friendly and tells us stories about the theatres and the actors. She says lots of girls come to London to become actresses, only some of them don't know anything about acting so they end up coming to no good or in the gutter and they can't all be taken on by a Royal Duke. Dear mother, *are you shocked at all this gossip. Everybody talks like this in London and everybody knows that the Royal Princes and Dukes mix freely with the actresses. Mrs. Bennet says we are lucky to have come to London already knowing what we are going to do and with the right connections, otherwise she would be concerned about our safety, so do not be worried, mother. Tomorrow we shall meet the other members of the company.**

London, 1772

... I am so excited that I can scarcely keep my pen straight on the paper in order to write this letter. Fanny, Sarah and I have today been privileged to listen to the voice of Miss Elizabeth Linley who is famous throughout London and who is said to be the most accomplished singer that this country has ever produced. She has been taught by her father in Bath, where he is organist and singing master. He has written music for plays by Mr. Sheridan, who has brought her and her sister, Mary, to London to sing in the theatre at Drury Lane. Mary has been telling us about the concerts in the great houses of Bath and Cheltenham, and about the Music Meetings in the towns of Gloucester, Worcester and Hereford, where she and Eliza have sung solo and chorus parts. She believes that some of us are due to go to Gloucester this year, but we wait to be told about that. At the present we meet daily to sing the new catches and glees and learn our parts in the choruses from the operas and oratorios, and some of our company will have the opportunity to sing solo items. It is very strange to think about you being so far away and

---

* A secondary group of musicians connected with the Noblemen and Gentlemen's Catch Club, an all male preserve founded in 1761 by the Earl of Sandwich who brought singers from Cambridge, the North and Leicestershire down to London for the purpose of performing glees, canons and catches. In the new company his male friends would provide the lower parts but the treble line was augmented by girls who were already familiar with musical notation. It is quite probable that some of these singers would have found work in the theatres as chorus singers in Operas and Oratorios by Handel. They would at any rate be well acquainted with the style of Handel's music as was the majority of the population of London.

home so different from the noise and dirt of London. There are many people here in Covent Garden and some of them are very poor, there is much gambling and drinking. The very rich folk have moved to new houses out of town where there are green fields and the air is cleaner. ...

We can go on a boat downstream to Greenwich or upstream to Richmond and see how the wealthy live in their grand houses. It makes us very sad when we come back to our lodgings and see the ragged children in the street. Fanny and I and the other girls seem to be living in the middle of the city where the whole world comes to talk about every subject under the sun. Some discuss politics till they are blue in the face, some worry about the poor folk, others gossip about the Royals and the latest play or opera. We are enjoying living here so much that we cannot imagine anything more entertaining or any better way of life, though I assure you dear mother that I miss you all most dreadfully.

Your loving daughter, Ellen.

London, September 1772

Dear Mother,
I may not be able to post this letter today because of being in such a hurry and a flurry with getting our bags packed.

Fanny caught her dress on the corner of a cart as we ran home through the market. You must not be worried about this though, we have woken very early this morning and she is mending while I write. I want to tell you everything that I see and hear while we are away from you. I know I won't remember it all when we come back home so I shall write it down now and put this account at the bottom of my bag to read it out to you when I come back. I am very fortunate to have been given some paper by Mr. Bennet, our land-lord. I think he feels he should look after us 'poor young ladies,' as he calls us, 'so far from home, and just to sing a few songs.'

Tomorrow will be Tuesday and we leave London. Our destination is Gloucester, but we must first make the journey on the Flying

Machine which departs from the Bell and Crown at five o'clock in the morning. Mr. Bennet will put our baggage on the hand cart to get us to Holborn and see us safely on the coach. Mrs. Bennet has promised to wake us in good time but I doubt if we shall sleep even a wink tonight with all the excitement. We shall be set down at the Bear Inn, in Oxford High Street in time for supper; here we shall stay overnight, or maybe for longer, and continue our journey by Post Chaise to Gloucester when everybody is gathered. All the performers are instructed to be settled in the town by Sunday so to be ready on Monday morning sharp for rehearsal of all the music that is to be played and sung at the Meeting ...

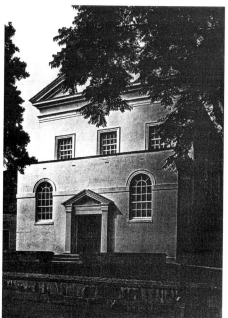

The oldest Music Room in Europe,
that in Holywell Lane, Oxford, opened in 1748

... I cannot find the words to describe Oxford, which is such a place of magnificent buildings, only glimpsed at from the coach as we came into the town. The road from London brought us over the brow of a hill and there, coming out of the mist that was just then settling in the valley and the sun going down behind it all, we could see churches and towers, spires and domes; the like of which I wouldn't ever have imagined if I had stayed at home all my life.

... On our first morning in Oxford we were invited to meet at the Music Room which is quite grand and well set out for concerts with an organ and space for about 200 people to attend. Here were assembled some of the party who are to travel to Gloucester. Mr. Giardini who will lead the band is from the Opera House in London and Mr. Malchair from Oxford will lead the second violins. They treated us to a concert all of our own with some of the pieces they are to play in Gloucester. It was the finest playing I have ever heard and I had to pinch myself to find out if I was really here. These two gentlemen have both been engaged many times by the Stewards of the Meetings and are well acquainted with each other and with many of the players from London as well as the singers from St. Paul's and the Chapel Royal. They must all have been wondering what six girls from the North were doing there, as I must confess, I was myself, but Mr. Malchair, realizing our discomfiture explained our situation to them and put us at our ease. Since then we have been assisted in every possible way by all the other singers and players in matters of where to present ourselves each day for the music and where to get food and drink, and to find our lodgings.

Mr. Malchair is so very amenable. He told us that when he first went to Hereford fourteen years ago it was to play for Messiah when it was to be put on in the Cathedral for the first time. He said that was because the Public Hall in the town was neither in a fit enough condition nor of a suitable size to accommodate all the players as well as the gathering who came to listen. It was a great honour to speak with this gentleman who knows so much about the Meetings and about the music that he plays every year.

... there is so much to tell you and we have so little time to ourselves now that we have at last arrived in Gloucester. We are very well cared for with a pleasant room in the centre of the town just

GLOCESTER, July 6, 1772.

The MUSICK MEETING

Of the Three Choirs of GLOCESTER, WORCESTER,
and HEREFORD,

Will be held at GLOCESTER, on Wednesday September 9, and the Two following Days.

ON Wednesday Morning will be performed at
the Cathedral, A TE DEUM and JUBILATE.
The Musick of which is taken from the most eminent
Italian Composers. Also Two of Mr. HANDEL's
CORONATION ANTHEMS, and an ORGAN CON-
CERTO by Mr. BRODERIP. In the Evening, at the
Booth-Hall, the Oratorio of JUDAS MACCABÆUS,
with a Solo on the Violin by Mr. Giardini; a Hautboy
Concerto by Mr. Fischer; and a Solo on the Violoncello
by Mr. Crosdale.

On Thursday Morning at the Cathedral the DETTIN-
GEN TE DEUM, JUBILATE, CORONATION-AN-
THEM, an ANTHEM composed by Mr. NORRIS, and
an ORGAN CONCERTO by Mr. BRODERIP. In the
Evening at the Booth-Hall, the Oratorio of JEPTHA; a
Solo by Mr. Giardini; a Concerto by Mr. Fischer; and a
Solo on the Violoncello by Mr. Crosdale.

On Friday Morning at the Cathedral, the MESSIAH.
In the Evening at the Booth-Hall a CONCERT, consisting of Full Pieces, some of the most admired Catches
and Glees, Solos, and Concertos by Messrs. GIARDINI,
FISCHER, and CROSDALE.

Principal Vocal Performers, Miss LINLEY, Miss M.
LINLEY, Miss RADCLIFFE, with others of the celebra-
ted Female Chorus Singers from the North of England,
Messrs. NORRIS, MATTHEWS, and PRICE. assisted by
the Rev. Mr. MAXEY, and several of the Clergy and
Gentlemen of the different Choirs. First Violin by Mr.
GIARDINI, the other Parts of the Instrumental Band by
the most approved Performers now in England.

N. B. The Chorusses, both Vocal and Instrumental, are
intended to be particularly full. The Whole to be conducted by Messrs. BRODERIP and ISAACS.

His Grace the Duke of BEAUFORT,
             A N D   } Stewards.
The Rev. Dr. TUCKER, Dean of Glocester,

The Performers, both Vocal and Instrumental, are re-
quested to be in Glocester on Sunday Evening, in order
to rehearse on Monday Morning at Ten o'Clock that Day,
and to dine with the Stewards at the Bell at Two.

*Jackson's Oxford Journal 1772. Notice of the Musick Meeting
with the first mention of the 'celebrated Female Chorus Singers
from the North of England'*

37

by the cathedral; and oh, what a wonderful sight this is. I wish I could describe it to you because there is nothing so fine and elegant anywhere else in England. Except that it is a great deal like some of the beautiful buildings that we saw in Oxford, being of the same light colour. You will never have seen such a stone. The sun seems to shine on the cathedral all the time even if everywhere else is dark; and the windows are full of the most vivid colours in the glass. The vaulting in the roof is quite beyond belief and even in the passage ways around the back there is decorated stone of the highest quality. I don't know how I am ever going to think about singing, there is so much to look at ...

Monday

Today has been very difficult. There are so many people here trying to play the same piece of music but in different ways ... we have spent the whole day in the college hall trying to get the notes together. ... for Messiah, Mr. Isaac has a different way of beating time from the way we were taught by Mr. Crompton and Mr. Stopford and we became quite lost several times. Fortunately, the cathedral singing men are familiar with his way and even the boys, although there are only ten of them, seem to be able to understand what is required so we must copy them. They have sweet voices but they are so few in numbers that they become overpowered by the other parts in the choruses

Tuesday

... we were so tired after the rehearsal which went on all day yesterday without seeming to improve the execution of the music, that Fanny was almost in tears and wanted to run back home. But we persuaded her to take a draught of ale and make certain of a good sleep and now she is better. We can have a leisurely time dressing this morning but are due to take breakfast with the Stewards at mid-day. The choir-men say this is the only time when

WORCESTER, July 19, 1773.

WORCESTER MUSIC-MEETING

WILL be held on Wednesday the Eighth of September, and the two following Days.

At the Cathedral, on Wednesday Morning, will be performed, a TE DEUM and JUBILATE, adapted to Music of the most eminent Italian Composers, a New ANTHEM, composed by Mr. Smith, and two of Mr. Handel's CORONATION ANTHEMS.

At the College Hall, in the Evening, the Oratorio of JOSHUA; a Solo on the Violin, by Mr. Giardini, and an Oboe Concerto, by Mr. Fischer.

At the Cathedral, on Thursday Morning, Handel's Dettingen TE DEUM, JUBILATE, and CORONATION ANTHEM, and a New ANTHEM, composed by Dr. Alcock.

At the College Hall, in the Evening, the Oratorio of JEPHTHA; a Violin Solo, by Mr. Giardini; and an Oboe Concerto, by Mr. Fischer.

At the Cathedral, on Friday Morning, MESSIAH.

At the Hall, in the Evening, a Grand MISCELLANEOUS CONCERT; consisting of capital Songs, Pieces for the Violin, by Mr. Giardini, for the Oboe, by Mr. Fischer, for the Violoncello, by Mr. Crosdil, and for the Clarionet, by Mr. Mahon.

Principal Vocal Performers,—Miss Linley, Miss Radcliffe, the celebrated Female Chorus Singers from the North of England, Messrs. Norris, Mathews, and Price, assisted by the Rev. Mr. Maxcy, and several of the Clergy and Gentlemen of the Choirs.

First Violin by Mr. Giardini; the other Parts of the Instrumental Band by the most approved Performers now in England.

The Choruffes are intended to be particularly full. The Whole to be conducted by Mr. Isaac.

The Right Hon. the Earl of Coventry
and
The Rev. Mr. Evans, Prebendary of Worcester,
} Stewards.

Notice in the Worcester Postman, *1773*

39

Hereford Music-Meeting.

HEREFORD, July 20.

The Meeting of the Three Choirs, of HEREFORD, GLOUCESTER, *and* WORCESTER, *for the Benefit of the* WIDOWS *and* ORPHANS *of the Poor* CLERGY *of the three Dioceses will be held at* HEREFORD, *on* WEDNESDAY *the 14th of* SEPTEMBER *and the two following Days.*

ON WEDNESDAY morning will be performed, at the Cathedral, Mr. Purcell's Te Deum and Jubilate, with Dr. Boyce's additions; an Anthem suitable to the occasion, by Dr. Boyce; and Mr. Handel's Coronation Anthem. In the evening, at the Music-Room, a Miscellaneous Concert.

On THURSDAY morning, at the Cathedral, Mr. Handel's Dettingen, Te Deum and Jubilate, and Coronation Anthem; and an Anthem by Dr. Boyce. In the evening, at the Music-Room, the Oratorio of JUDAS MACCABEUS.

On FRIDAY morning, at the Cathedral, The MESSIAH, a sacred Oratorio, to which none will be admitted without Tickets. In the evening, at the Music-Room, a Grand Miscellaneous Concert.

After each evening's performance will be a Ball, to which no person will be admitted without a Concert Ticket.

Tickets to be had (Price 5s. 3d. each) of Mr. Pugh and Mr. Badham, at the Swan and Falcon, and at the Green Dragon.

Principal performers: The celebrated Miss Davis, Mrs. Wrighten, Miss Radcliff, and the Female Chorus Singers from the North, Messrs. Norris and Mathews, Sigrs. Giardini, Fischer, Malchari, Parke, Crosdil, &c. &c.

The performers are desired to be in town on Sunday evening, in order to rehearse on Monday the 12th in the morning, and to dine with the Stewards at the Swan and Falcon the day following.

UVEDALE PRICE, Esq.
AND THE
Rev. Mr. ARCHDEACON CLIVE, } Stewards.

There will be an Ordinary on Wednesday at the Green Dragon, and on Thursday at the Swan and Falcon.

Notice in the Hereford Journal, *1774*

40

*we are permitted to speak with the gentry - as these Stewards surely
are - since they are fulfilling one of their duties by welcoming all the
performers on the first day of the Meeting. But I will not know what
to say to them. I have no knowledge of their kind of life and I doubt
if they know anything about spinning.*

Wednesday

*... this evening there is a concert in the Boothall of Mr. Handel's
oratorio Judas Maccabaeus with a solo on the violin by Mr. Giardini
and a hautboy concerto played by Mr. Fisher. Tomorrow evening the
oratorio Jephtha in the Boothall with a solo by Mr. Giardini and a
concerto by Mr. Fisher. Also the services in the cathedral in the
mornings when two of Mr. Handel's Coronation Anthems will be
sung by the Choirs of the three cathedrals as well as organ
concertos by Mr. Broderip, but the finest music ever written will be
performed in the cathedral on Friday morning when all the singers
from the three cities, besides those from London, Oxford and 'the
celebrated female chorus singers from the North of England' as we
are now called, will together perform Messiah.*

*After that there is advertized a Miscellaneous Concert. There will
be the latest Glees and Catches from London, Songs from operas and
solos and concertos played on the violin, hautboy and violoncello.
Our heads are spinning already.*

Ellen's first visit to Gloucester in 1772 was followed in subsequent years by
those to Worcester and Hereford. Her idols, the Linley sisters from Bath, still
teenagers like herself, were at the height of their fame, and their style of
singing, small and sweet, was copied by all aspiring soloists. For six years,
Sarah Harrop was one of the chorus singers but in 1778 came to Gloucester
as a soloist. Many of the girls who took the annual journey from the
provinces to London for the opera season must have hoped to reach these
dizzy heights, and indeed some of them were appointed 'leader' or 'principal' of the group, sometimes taking on the role of solo singer in the
Miscellaneous Concerts. Over the years the names of Miss Radcliffe, Mrs.
Shepley, Miss Harwood and Miss Russell occur, all of whom appear to have

come from Halifax and Leeds, and to have been taught by the organists, Mr. Crompton, Mr. Stopford or Mr. Jobson.

It is interesting to note other connections between southern England with, in particular, Leeds and Halifax, showing the level which cultural activities had reached in Yorkshire. Players from the Yorkshire theatre often moved on to Drury Lane, Covent Garden and thence to Bath and Cheltenham; in fact, strolling players were in evidence at the early 18th century Three Choirs Meetings, providing entertainment of all sorts, to suit all tastes and all classes throughout the towns—an early fringe event.

Mr. Linley senior was a renowned organist in Bath, but another musician who came to Bath from Leeds and Halifax where he had been organist at the parish churches and directed concerts that included their first hearings of Messiah was William Herschel, originally from Hanover, later to become Astronomer Royal to George III.

With all this activity going on in London, Leeds and Bath, it is rather touching to come to the smallest of the Three Choirs cities, Hereford and read in Grove's *Dictionary of Music and Musicians* that it was 'too small and remote to develop much public musical life'! Thank God for the Three Choirs Festival.

Grove does go on to say, 'However, the members of the College of Vicars Choral and their friends performed a good deal of secular ensemble music among themselves.' This might seem to be unfair dismissal of Hereford, since, apart from there being an everlasting problem of finding enough financial backing for concerts in so small a city, the enthusiasm for the Music Meetings, the appreciation of a high standard of performance, and the welcome always extended to the visiting artists and the thousands of listeners who have come to this town again and again, demonstrate an awareness of the true value of the Art sometimes difficult to find in the sophistication of larger towns.

One last letter gives us a picture of Hereford.

1777

Dear Mother,
We are come again to Hereford and find that Mrs. Thackray has our room all ready for us. She makes us very welcome and it is almost like coming home. We have stayed in so many houses over the years in London, Oxford, Gloucester, Worcester and Hereford. Sometimes

I forget where I am, that is, until I look at the cathedrals, being so very different one from another. Do you remember how I was quite overwhelmed by the height and size of Gloucester's Cathedral? Hereford is so different. The stone is dark pink; I have never seen such colour as this before, and the style of the building is more broad and solid, having a feeling of warmth and homeliness. There are towers and spires above the main body of the cathedral but without the fine decoration to be seen at Gloucester and at Worcester. The town is small and the cathedral looks over the little houses and shops. The public buildings are not very good but just by the cathedral there is a fine Music Room in the style of that found in Oxford. The concerts take place here or in the cathedral.

Artist's impression of the Music Room at Hereford (© K. Kimber)

It is very fortunate that our landlord is a draper as our dresses are in sore need of repair and replacement. Some of the girls have purchased cloth and Mrs. Thackray has already said she will make it up.

The music will be much like other years of the Music Meeting. We have our parts in Mr. Handel's Alexander's Feast and there will be airs and choruses by Mr. Boyce, and Mr. Rauzzini. On the last day Mr. Handel's Messiah will be performed in the cathedral as has become the custom. We now know this piece well enough not to be bothered by the conductor's ill temper at rehearsal. I always think of Mr. Malchair when we sing Messiah because he was so helpful to us when we were newly in the chorus. He doesn't come any more, neither does Mr. Giardini. The new leader of the band is from Vienna. At the special services in the cathedral the choirs sing anthems by Handel, Boyce, and Purcell. Last year they sang one by Dr. Howard and the year before one by Miss Linley's brother Thomas. It is very fine to hear our friends' music being sung in the cathedrals.

The gentry in Hereford are not as glittering as we saw at Worcester, though the balls that follow the evening concerts go on quite as long, if not longer. In fact we have heard that people were still dancing at 4 o'clock in the morning! Perhaps that is why they go to sleep during the concerts. We do not attend any of these balls of course but we can see the arrival of the ladies and gentlemen and the dresses are spectacular. The Ladies place a cushion on their heads and comb the front hair over it to meet the back, all to make them appear taller. It certainly makes them hold their backs straight. Their hooped petticoats are very wide at the hem and of the most beautiful colours, imitating the French fashion. The Gentlemen have gold and silver decorations on their coats and cocked hats. We are more reserved in our mode of dress since it would not be fitting for us to call attention to ourselves.

7 Just Good Friends

Music, the greatest good that mortals know
And all of heaven we have below.
From 'Song for St. Cecilia's Day' by Joseph Addison

Very early on in its history, the chorus associated with the Music Meetings had a different tonal quality from that of a cathedral choir, due to the imported voices.

The works mentioned below are the major ones in which the chorus would have participated.[1]

1772 (G) Jephtha, Judas Maccabaeus, Messiah, Misc; Concert. 'In addition [to the Linley sisters, Mary and Elizabeth] were engaged this year for the first time to assist the trebles in the choruses, Miss Radcliffe and others of the celebrated female chorus singers, as they were called, from the North of England.' Miss Radcliffe later came as Mrs. Russell bringing with her a sister-in-law, Miss Russell.

1773 (W) Joshua, Jephtha, Messiah, Misc; Concert. 'Vocal performers at this meeting were Miss Mary Linley, Miss Radcliffe, and other female chorus singers from the North of England; Norris, Matthews and Price [Boy trebles], and the clergy and gentlemen of the Three Choirs.'

1774 (H) Judas Maccabaeus, Messiah, Two Misc; Concerts. 'The other female singers were Mrs. Wrighten, a vocal performer of considerable eminence at Drury Lane Theatre and Vauxhall; Miss Radcliffe and the chorus-singers from the North.'

The Yorkshire Post mentioned that 'It was common from 1770 to transport the women singers of Lancashire and Yorkshire for the great performances of London, The Birmingham Festival and The Three Choirs Meetings.'

1783 (H) 'Miss Harwood, brought forward by Miss Harrop, was principal singer of the Ancient Concerts in London and at the Festival of the Three Choirs of Worcester, Gloucester and Hereford. She had been a pupil of Mr. Jobson of Leeds Parish Church and furnished the first instance of a vocalist who, having received her instruction in the provinces, was immediately engaged to appear as a principal (solo) singer in the first (major) concerts in London.' (*Halifax Guardian*).

Mr. Jobson, in his turn had been one of the singers at Halifax Parish Church in one of the very early performances of Messiah in 1766, at which William Herschel played the organ but immediately after that event Jobson was appointed organist in Halifax.

It appears from the *Annals of the Three Choirs* that soon after 1784, the year of the Handel Commemoration Concerts in Westminster Abbey, those of the Meetings degenerated somewhat into 'Selections from ...' and 'Miscellaneous Concerts'. For many years Messiah was the only major work to be performed in its entirety.

Haydn's Creation, first heard in Vienna in 1798, came to Covent Garden in 1800 but even this work, after its Three Choirs debuts in 1800, 1801 & 1802, was reduced to 'parts of' or 'selections from'. Chorus parts were still sung by the three cathedral choirs augmented by the northern ladies and occasional men from Oxford, Cambridge, Norwich, and the London cathedrals, on their way to becoming soloists themselves.

One of these gentlemen was a Mr. Vaughan, a lay-clerk from Norwich, who came in 1800 for the performance of the Creation. Miss Tennant also came that year and by 1805 these two were married. This husband and wife team continued their singing work for many years, Mrs. Vaughan hardly stopping even when the birth of her children was imminent; in fact, her appearance at Gloucester in 1811 was only cancelled at the very last minute when the baby came earlier than expected. Mr. Vaughan was a fine tenor, who, having served his apprenticeship in the chorus appeared as soloist in the first performance in London of Beethoven's Choral Symphony.

Another of the chorus sopranos was Catherine Stephens, 1794-1882, a Londoner, who was known for her sweetness of voice and temperament. She sang in oratorios at Covent Garden and Drury Lane theatres and came to the

CONCERTS

OF

ANTIENT MUSIC

UNDER THE PATRONAGE OF

THEIR MAJESTIES

AS PERFORMED AT THE

NEW ROOMS, HANOVER SQUARE.

1807

LONDON:

PRINTED FOR W. LEE,
by D N SHURY, BERWICK STREET, SOHO.

LIST OF PERFORMERS

VOCAL PERFORMERS

PRINCIPAL SINGERS

Mrs VAUGHAN
Mrs ASHE and **Mrs MOUNTAIN**
Mr HARRISON
Mr KNYVETT, Mr SALE,
Mr SALE, jnr. Mr GORE, Mr ELLIOTT,
Mr GOSS; and **Mr BARTLEMAN.**

CANTO CHORUS	ALTO CHORUS
Mrs SHEPLEY	Mr HORSEFALL
Miss TRAVIS	Mr WALKER
Miss SMITHERS	Mr KENDRICK
EIGHT CHAPEL ROYAL BOYS	Mr TERRY
FOUR ABBEY BOYS	Mr THOMAS
MASTER HEDGELEY	Mr JENKS
MASTER JONES	Mr PARS
	Mr SALMON, Jnr.

Concerts of Antient Music. Most of these singers performed at Three Choirs

Three Choirs Meetings for several years from 1807, latterly taking the principal parts. When she was 44 she married the Earl of Exeter (1758-1839) who was then aged 80. He died the next year leaving her a wealthy widow. The Earl was greatly involved in music-making and in 1778 is reported in a letter from Henry Bates, father of Joah, as having come to Cambridge to collect

---

UNDER THE DIRECTION OF

THE EARL OF DARTMOUTH
CONCERT OF ANCIENT MUSIC

WEDNESDAY FEBRUARY 4TH 1807

ACT I

CORONATION ANTHEM	Zadock the priest	Handel
DUET	Qual Andante	Marcello
CHORUS	Gloria in excelsis	Pergolesi
SONG	Gentle Morpheus (Alcides)	Handel
SESTETTO	In braccio ad te (Justin)	Handel
QUARTETTO & CHORUS	Then Round (Samson)	Handel
CONCERTO	(from select harmony)	Handel
SONG & CHORUS	Come if you (King Arthur)	Purcell
RECIT	Ye sacred priests	
SONG	Farewell ye limpid (Jephtha)	Handel
PSALM XVIII	St. Matthew Tune	Dr. Croft

ACT II

OVERTURE	(Rodelinda)	Handel
MADRIGAL	Since First I saw you	Ford
RECIT	Great Queen	
SONG	Gentle Airs (Athalia)	Handel
CHORUS	Venus Laughing (Theodore)	Handel
SONG	(From tyrannic love)	Purcell
CONCERTO 30th	(Grand)	Handel
SONG	Lord to thee (Theodore)	Handel
GRAND CHORUS	Hallelujah (Messiah)	Handel

A programme dominated by the music of Handel

48

Sarah and Joah to take them back with him to Burghley, Leicestershire, for concerts. The musical world in the late 18th century was indeed a small one.

1809 (W) The Creation Part I, Messiah, Selection of Sacred Music, Misc; Concerts. 'with chorus singers from Lancashire, Birmingham, Lichfield, and Bristol.'

1812 (W) Part of The Creation, Messiah. 'The band numbered 54 and the chorus 110, which, with the principal singers, gave a total of 174 performers.'

1818 (W) A special gallery was built at the east end of the cathedral to seat many more people.

Many performers are known to have come to the Festival year after year. They must have felt at home in the atmosphere of the cathedral towns, making friends with the townsfolk and enjoying reunions with their fellow musicians on familiar territory. Two of them, William and Deborah Knyvett, demonstrate remarkable staying powers and allegiance to the concert circuit which included the Meetings. Deborah Travis (1796-1876) first came as a chorus girl aged about 17. She was a native of Shaw and had, with her aunt Sarah, sung from the age of eight in several oratorio concerts in Todmorden and Shaw churches. Having been heard by Mr. Thomas Greatorix when he was conducting a concert in Manchester in which she and her aunt were singing. she was offered an apprenticeship for five years with the 'Antient Concerts Society in London, being bound by Indentures to H.R.H. the Duke of Cambridge.'[2]

In 1818 Deborah made her debut as a soloist in one of the miscellaneous concerts and continued as a member of the chorus or as a soloist for another 20 years. She met her future husband at the Meetings and became Mrs. Knyvett in 1826. In spite of having left her native town and mingled with those of a different up-bringing and station in life, she always kept contact with her friends and family back in Shaw, Crompton and Todmoden and supported two unmarried sisters and a brother in their old age.

William Knyvett, 1779-1856, came from Norfolk and was a descendant of the captor of Guy Fawkes and, more immediately, the son of the organist of the Chapel Royal. At the age of nine he was enrolled as a treble in the chorus of the Ancient Concerts, and later as one of the gentlemen of the King's Chapel, 'a most chaste counter-tenor, whose enunciation of the words of the English language has never been surpassed.' He too came to the Meetings initially as a member of the chorus and sometimes soloist, his name first appearing in 1799. His anthem was included in the programme for 1823. Mr. and Mrs. Knyvett were regular singers at the Meetings until 1838, during which time William became secretary of the London Catch Club, and with his father Charles, presented concerts in London. He conducted the Birmingham Festival from 1834 - 1843 and the York Festival in 1835, forging with those cities some useful ties which were to be maintained by the visits of further generations of choral singers in future years.

1824 (W) Messiah and selections from Judas Maccabaeus. 'The strength of the band and chorus was considerably increased, the total number being 156.'
   'The noble gallery was so admired that it was thrown open to sightseers on the Sunday prior to the Festival and great anticipations were entertained of the brilliant effect it will have when crowded with beauty and fashion—obviously a reference to the audience who were still being squeezed into the chancel. This proved inadequate for the crowds of people who wanted to see what as going on and during the Wednesday night of the 1827 Meeting, two further galleries were specially built.'[3]

1834 (H) The seating included a raised platform in the centre of the western aisle as well as seats on the floor and in the side aisles. Comment was made 'on the splendid appearance of the beautiful females [could this be the chorus?] who this time took their seats on the raised plane which were so admirably contrived that all could take their places without trouble and confusion and could see and be seen.'[4]

1836 (W) Mozart's Requiem (disguised as 'Redemption', in English with added words.), Messiah, Spohr's Last Judgement. 'This Meeting, which lasted four days, commenced on the 27th September with ... a band and chorus of 164 performers.'

1838 (G) Mendelssohn's St. Paul, Part of Creation, Messiah. 'This Meeting (or Festival as it now was designated on the programme) commenced on the 11th September ... The preparations for it were on a scale far exceeding any precedent afforded by former years. The numbers engaged were: 10 principal singers, 110 band & 181 chorus; making a total of 301 performers.' 'On the side of the nave, now in use for a second time, rose a splendid orchestra, affording easy accommodation for 300 performers ... level with the gallery

Nave of Hereford Cathedral on Wednesday 27th September 1837,
during a performance of the Messiah

and as high as the foot of the organ, which formed the background of the picture. The seats were decorated with scarlet cloth, which with the scarlet and gold ornamental work on the fronts of the gallery, formed a rich and bold contrast with the nave and its massive columns.'[5]

1842 (W) Messiah Judas Maccabaeus, Beethoven's Mount of Olives (disguised as 'Engedi'), Alexander's Feast, Haydn's Seasons, miscellaneous selection of arias, concertos and solos. '218 in the chorus, a total of 313 performers ... Mr. Joseph Surman of Exeter Hall engaged as conductor ... Judas Maccabaeus was, on the whole, exceedingly well rendered, the chorus, most of whom were from Exeter Hall, being thoroughly familiar with that work.'

Exeter Hall in the Strand, London, was opened in 1831 for religious meetings and for oratorio concerts, as well as a centre for the teaching of sight-singing. John Hullah, 1812-1884, born in Worcester, taught singing there for some time using a Sol-fa method.

A group of early 19th century soloists and choralists, in the dress of the day

8   At a Solemn Music

In Perfect Diapason
John Milton

The singers of the Annual Meetings of the Three Choirs of Hereford, Gloucester and Worcester at the end of the 18th century had been the men and boys of the three cathedral choirs, assisted and augmented by additional voices from St. Paul's Cathedral, The Chapel Royal, Oxford, and the girls from Halifax and Leeds. This state of affairs continued for another hundred years, with some variation in the sources of men's voices and some increase in the numbers of trebles, eventually to include singers from Oldham, Bradford, Huddersfield, Lichfield, Bristol, Norwich, Birmingham and Cambridge; though generally not all at the same time! The history books tell of a chorus of 44 in 1780 and 50 in 1788.

These same singers were much in demand throughout the country due to their thorough knowledge of the music, and their good fortune in having been trained by the best musicians of the day. At the 1784 Commemoration of Handel's Life and Work held in Westminster Abbey the performers numbered 526, a fairly unwieldy mass of musicians, increased in 1785 to over 600 and in 1786 to more than 800. This programme of Handel's music established another tradition—the annual performance of Messiah, parts of Messiah, or at least an aria or two, with 'The trumpet shall sound' and the 'Hallelujah Chorus', a habit still part of Christmas fare today.

Countrywide enthusiasm stirred up by the Handel commemoration concerts led eventually to the birth of that great British institution, the Choral Society. Music Clubs, to begin with an all male affair, existing to promote the performance of Madrigals, Glees and Rounds solely for their own entertainment, now took on the role of teaching the members to read the dots (notes on the stave) and eventually to perform them for the general public.

The Huddersfield Choral Society, since the end of the nineteenth century one of the best-known in the country for its 'Big Sound', its name conjuring up an impression of largely well-endowed ladies, men to match and a healthy vibrato in all quarters, was begun in 1836 as a music club and to start with the meetings were exclusively for members to sing and learn oratorios. Practices were held once a month at the time of the full moon, for the sake of those walking some distance back home. Male members paid 2s 6d, ladies nothing, both being allowed at every meeting three gills of ale and bread & cheese.

William Gardiner, born in 1770, a Leicester stocking manufacturer and excellent cellist played for a performance of Messiah in Huddersfield and wrote of it in his collection of reminiscences c.1830, entitled Music and Friends. 'The voices were manufacturers and weavers of the neighbourhood. The choristers, though good musicians, exhibited very little taste in the pronunciation of their words. They were accurate in their time, and pretty firm in their tone, which in their estimation were the only essentials in music ... With respect to their pronunciation there was much to excuse, as their language is barbarous and uncouth to the extreme.'

In Halifax there is anecdotal evidence of a well established choral tradition cutting across social boundaries before the emergence of the Halifax Choral Society in 1817. Although there are references to a music club in 1767, the earliest surviving records of institutionalised musical activity date from 1792 when the Philharmonic Society was founded.

In 1836 Hereford Philharmonic Society was formed consisting mainly of instrumentalists. In their rules and regulations they are asked to assist the choral society at their special meetings, so either there must have been some sort of band of singers already in operation, or else this is an ambiguous reference to the choir at the Three Choirs Meetings. The city's choral society started officially in 1837. Gloucester's choral society was in existence by 1845, and that of Worcester was founded in 1861 with the express purpose of providing singers for the Triennial Festivals. From 1848 local singers from the three cities had been invited to join the Festival Chorus.

Since, at the beginning of the 19th century few people could read music, the teaching and learning of the notes must have been 'listen and copy' or 'follow the chap next to you', both very dangerous practices which require a quick ear, great concentration and a lot of faith on the part of the singers and limitless patience from the chorus master. Some singers used the Sol-Fa system, sometimes called Old English Sol-Fa or Lancashire Sol-Fa, the latter title providing yet another indication of northern musical activity. Books were written on this method which in spite of its limitations was a help to new recruits to the choral scene. In the early 19th century it was invaluable as a means of sight-singing and entirely suitable for the repertoire of the young choral society. In the compositions of today with strange enharmonic key changes, or no key at all to fix upon, it has to a large extent been laid aside, although some do still use a rudimentary knowledge to help in pitching unexpected intervals.

There was a young lady of Norwich—no, this is not a limerick—called Sarah Ann Glover (1785-1867) who, taking the old Sol-Fa system, devised her own method of naming the notes Doh, re, mi, fa, soh, la, te, doh; Doh being the Key note at any one time. A congregational minister in Norwich, Rev. Curwen, born in Yorkshire, between Halifax and Leeds, was not a musician but wished to improve Sunday-school singing. He had no knowledge of musical notation so in 1841 consulted Miss Glover on the matter. He copied and perfected her ideas and from 1844 when he moved to London, set up a college of music, a music society and a publishing firm, the latter in 1863, for carrying on this work. Armed with this system, elementary school teachers who had themselves no real musical education were able to do successful sight-reading work and artisans became efficient choralists. The result was an almost overnight appearance of a class of musically literate people to whom the great choral works were accessible. Musical appreciation and taste probably came later but at least the singers now had a language to read. An article in the *Musical Times* in 1887 recalls 1840, when 'with curiosity excited everywhere, and hopes flattered on all hands, the desire to study music spread like a wave over the country, affecting secluded hamlets, as well as conspicuous cities. Few were exempt from its influence. Young and old went sol-faing and even the prejudices of class were in many cases broken down by a common desire to sing with understanding.'

Books of Hymns and Psalms were written using this method and to this day there are singers who were brought up on Messiah in Tonic Sol-Fa. Their rendering of:

> For un-to us a child is bo-rn
> S. d. d. f. f. f. f. - m.

can send us into fits of laughter nowadays but must have been a very serious matter, particularly when they came to the semi-quavers, a positive tongue-twister.

No. 12.   CHORUS.—FOR UNTO US A CHILD IS BORN.

Doh is **G**. *Andante Allegro*. M. 76.

[Tonic Sol-fa musical notation]

A
p SOPRANO.

For un-to us a Child is born, un - to us a Son is

giv-en, un - to us a Son is giv-en, *p* TENOR. For un - to

for un - to us a Child is born:
us a Child is born, un - to us a Son is

B   D.t.
p ALTO. For un -to

giv-en, un - to us a Son is giv-en:

us a Child is born, un - to us a Son is

p BASS. For un - to us a Child is born,

Chorus from Messiah, in Tonic Sol-fa notation

Choral societies sprang up in most towns and cities throughout Britain from 1818 onwards, at first to reproduce the Handel commemoration concerts in London, but later in order to present their own choice of programme. The idea of an annual Music Festival, or as in the case of Birmingham, a triennial one, had been realized before the end of the 18th century, although the Three Choirs Meetings were not called Festivals until 1838.

56

The northern towns had a head-start when it came to singing, since there was already a strong tradition of communal music-making amongst the spinners and weavers. Add to this the Industrial Revolution and its repercussions in the lives of the workers, producing a desperate craving for relief from the conditions of factory work, for recreation of the mind and soul after tending machines all day:

The Hand-loom Weaver's Lament

So, come all you cotton-weavers, you must rise up very soon,
For you must work in factories from morning until noon:
You mustn't walk in your garden for two or three hours a day,
For you must stand at their command, and keep your shuttles play.
From *Ballads and Songs of Lancashire*

Then imagine the healing effect that singing would have had. There is no better exercise for the lungs than having to breathe deeply and control the release of air. There is no better exercise for the brain than having to read, listen and organize the vocal chords all at the same time. There is no better exercise for the spirit than to be with like minded people striving to make musical harmony.

Hand in hand with the emergence of groups of people wanting to sing together came the establishment of publishers who could guarantee that everybody had the same dots or symbols, something which wouldn't have always been the case when all music was copied by hand. Vincent Novello began publishing music in 1811 and his son Alfred built up a business which is still closely associated with choral music.

It seems ironic that, at a time when all the resources were coming together—growing populations of exhausted factory workers and aspiring singers, improved printing, a developing railway system making travel easier between towns, and better educational opportunities for the working classes—there just wasn't very much good new music for them to sing, apart from works by Handel. In fact public taste seems to have degenerated somewhat over the first half of the 19th century and although the early choral societies maintained performances of Messiah, there were few British composers apparently able and willing to write for them. Maybe it was still a class problem. Music and the other arts had been patronized by and produced for

57

the nobility, not for the working classes. It needed a shift of direction to focus on the masses instead of on the king and his courtiers. The kind of entertainment suitable for Hanoverian Royalty who might wish to talk or even eat during a performance was not going to appeal to the mill workers of Halifax and Leeds with their thirst for improving their new-found skills in harmony, or for their more down-to-earth approach to letting their hair down on a Saturday night.

Another facet of urban life shows a picture of music purely for entertainment to be found in pubs and the music hall. The labourer loved it as a relaxation after a hard day's work but social reformers were disturbed at the amount of drink and disorderliness that accompanied it. In many a hostelry, patrons who enjoyed playing riotous music and singing bawdy songs on Saturday, changed, with equal verve, to hymn singing on Sundays. Their neighbours, maintaining the air of respectability by observing the Sabbath, deploring the evils of drink and on Sundays banning all reading of books other than the Bible, were singing the same hymns in the church next door. Just as incongruous to the audience of today are the programmes for concerts or 'selections' given in public halls to the more élite listener and to be found in early Three Choirs programmes. These were a list of solo and choral items, glees and madrigals, hymns and street ballads, culled from opera house, church, music hall, the high street, and parlour and without much allowance being made for continuity of meaning or verbal content. The audience went away satisfied provided there was a chorus from an oratorio to finish with.

Mill owners, churchmen and town councils were keen to encourage controlled singing of sacred music because it was considered that in so doing, the rabble would be kept on the straight and narrow path to goodness.

9 Intermezzo

Let all the world in every corner sing.

From 'Antiphon' by George Herbert

Meanwhile the contingents of northern singers kept on coming every year to the West Country bringing with them their own distinctive bright, clear, positive type of voice production which carried well in cathedral and public halls. Without ruffling any feathers by taking a sideways step onto a different platform, remember the vocal strength and clarity of the late Gracie Fields, a native of Rochdale, some four miles from Shaw. Was this the singing voice of the area? If so, the six girls who were taken to London and beyond would certainly have deserved the title 'Celebrated Female Singers from the North'. All sacred music sung in the cathedrals would, until 1834, have been performed in the chancel, shut off from the main body of the church and quite private, with not much hope of any words being heard in the rest of the building, so maybe that is why help was needed, especially for Messiah. Anybody who has had to sing behind a stone archway knows what it feels like.

Miscellaneous Concerts became longer and longer with solos, choruses, concertos and excerpts from oratorios by Handel, Boyce, Spohr and others, but the style of programme planning left much to be desired compared with the present day. Adulation of the soloist produced the patchwork of songs sung by the same prima donnas year after year, interspersed with instrumental pieces and choruses from Messiah, Judas Maccabaeus or Jephtha; a list of unconnected items lacking the message of the full oratorio. In fact these concerts became not so much a musical experience as an aperitif to the Grand

Ball which followed; an indication that the popularity of the social side of the Festival seems to have gone up while the standard of music declined. Watkins Shaw says in his book on the Festival, 'No other English festival of those years [referring to the 1860s] can produce such a staggering list of moribund works of the oratorio pattern.'

Such was the pinnacle of non-achievement as far as programme making was concerned, but at least the Three Choirs did keep going on its thin musical diet; the singers and players doing their best to create something beautiful and the audiences coming from far and wide. In all fairness we have to bear in mind the difficulty of finding works suitable for cathedral performance until those of Parry started to revitalize the English Oratorio tradition. Generally composers from other countries were busy writing operatic or instrumental music, or else they were Catholic and wrote for a form of religious thought unacceptable to the Church of England of the day.

Fortunately, Haydn's Creation arrived in 1800, sowing the seed for what was to come 100 years later and maintaining the Oratorio as the foundation of our programmes. What went on around these oratorios and indeed even in the middle of them when they were butchered and served up in cutlets at the secular concerts, seems to be something of a musical muddle, but the audience enjoyed it. Apparently nobody's hair stood on end when 'Auld Robin Grey', a popular parlour ballad, was sung between 'I know that my redeemer liveth' and 'Hallelujah'.

The programmes were inordinately long and the audience were invited to 'feel free to leave the room between the musical items'. The atmosphere would certainly not have been conducive to sustained concentration, but one could chat with friends.

Looking at these vast programmes for the Miscellaneous Concerts, I wonder if the chorus girls and boys had to learn it all by heart, for if so, it would have been a veritable memory marathon; if not then how did they cope with all the song sheets? Were they drilled in platform behaviour and warned on pain of dismissal not to fidget or drop a single piece of paper? Very few records of these early 19th century programmes exist, and even less about the choirs, but we do know that the gentry flocked to the secular concerts in such numbers that windows had to be removed in order to let in air and ladies were asked to wear less voluminous dresses so that more people could gain admittance. They were also asked to remove their hats! How was this request received? For the leisured county families the annual Meetings with parties, receptions and balls were a chance to gather and seek out partners for their

A Grand Selection of Sacred Music

PART I

Overture and Dead March from Saul		Handel
Recitation and Song, "It must be so" and "pour forth no more"		Handel
	Mr. Bartleman	
Chorus, "No more to Ammon's God"		
Song, "O magnify the Lord"	Miss Williams	
Recit. and song, "Why does the God of Israel"	Mr. Vaughan	
Chorus, "Gird on thy sword"		
Recit. and Song, "O worse than death" and "Angles ever bright and fair"		Handel
	Miss Stephens	
Recit. "And God said"	Mr. Vaughan	
Chorus "The heavens are telling"		Haydn

PART II

Recit. "These as they change" and Air	Mr. Bartleman	Calcott
Chorus, "O God who in thy heavenly hand" (Joseph		Handel
Recit. "S willed my father"	Mr. Vaughan	Handel
Luther's Hymn		
Recit. and Song "Ye sacred priests" "Farewell ye limpid streams"		Handel
	Miss Stephens	
Grand Chorus, "Hallelujah (Mount of Olives)		Beethoven

PART III

Introduction and Chorus, "Ye sons of Israel"		Handel
Recit. and Song, "My cup is full" "Shall I in Maure's"		Handel
	Mr. Bartleman	
Chorus, "For all these mercies"		
Song, "Let the bright Seraphim"	Miss Stephens	Handel
Chorus, "Let their celestial concerts"		
Song, "Lord remember david"	Mr. Vaughan	Handel
Double Chorus, "The Lord shall reign"		Handel

The Miscellaneous Concert from the Hereford programme of 1816

A MORNING CONCERT
PART I

Opening Movement	Te Deum	Graun
Recit. and Air	What tho' I trace	Handel
Duett	Qual Anelante	Marcello
Quartett	For this God	Marcello & Knyvett
Recit. and Air	O liberty	Handel
	From mighty kings	Handel
	Shall I in Mamre's	Handel
Chorus	For all these mercies	Handel
Recit. and Air	With verdure clad	Haydn
Recit.	In splendour bright	Haydn
Chorus	The heavens are telling	Haydn

PART II

First Grand Concerto		Handel
Offertorio	The Hymn	Dr. Chard
Chorus	Kyrie Eleison	Riglimi
Air	Agnus Dei	Mozart
Chorus	Rex Tremendae	Winter
Quartett	Recordare	Winter
Chorus	Lachrymosa	Winter
Air	Gratias agimus	Guglielmi
Recit. and Air	The snares of death	Stevenson
Recit.	So willed my father	Handel
Trio and Chorus	Disdainful of danger	Handel
Chorus	If guiltless blood	Handel
Chorus	Cum Sancto Spiritu	Mozart

Part III

Luther's Hymn		
Air	O magnify the Lord	Handel
Scena	The last man	Calcott
Recit. and Aria	Ah! Parlate	Cimarosa
Chorus	Glory be to God	Beethoven
Air	O my God	Ciampi
Quartetto	Domine Jesu Christi	Winter
Chorus	The Lord shall reign	Handel

A Morning Concert in Gloucester on 23rd September 1829,
which would have left little time for anything else that day

unattached offspring before the winter hunting season began and while horse and carriage could still pass along the unmetaled roads, so part of the fun was in dressing to the latest fashion.

All this would have been noticed with fascination and amusement by the members of the chorus from their vantage point on the platform. Without

The collapsed west front of Hereford Cathedral in 1786, showing the Music Room to the right. (An engraving from a drawing by James Wathen)

doubt many of the audience attended concerts in order to be noticed. That ambition was achieved, but I am sure they didn't really have the members of the chorus in mind when they dressed up for their appearances in Guildhall, Shirehall or College Hall. As far as the gentry were concerned, musicians were servants, as in the previous century, and in fact often came from the working class, so their opinions did not need to be considered. No self respecting young person of the middle class would have dreamt of appearing on the stage unless they wished to be disowned by their parents, but for the singers it was a great step up in the world, and a chance to witness the behaviour of the wealthy, although not to mingle.

The Music Room in Hereford (see illustrations previous page and p.43), built in the 1760s and noted by Ellen in her diary to be so fine and like those of Oxford, was only slightly damaged on Easter Monday, 1786 when the West end of Hereford Cathedral collapsed. This room is referred to by another

writer in 1810 as 'a huge ugly brick building erected for the music', which shows how within 50 years taste can change course dramatically in matters architectural as well as in other spheres. It was demolished in 1835 anyway and one hopes that there was a genuine 'structurally unsound' reason rather than mere whim.

The Guildhall in Worcester, an elegant building still standing in Foregate St. has been the scene of many a discussion over the suitability of music, venue, programme, dress, concert and soloist, and eventually was abandoned by the Three Choirs as a concert hall in favour

The Guildhall, Worcester

of College Hall, itself a truly magnificent building suitable for any social gathering.

In Gloucester the Booth Hall was used until 1817 when the Shire Hall was opened. All these halls were, until the 1830s considered more suitable for the performances of oratorio other than Messiah than were the cathedrals, since

The Booth Hall, Westgate Street, Gloucester, demolished in 1957

oratorios had received their first airings in theatres in London and people associated them with the naughty ways of the actors rather than with the decorous ways of the dean. The chorus work was taken on by contingents of visiting singers in ever increasing numbers, 110 at Worcester in 1812, 119 at Gloucester in 1835, until by 1838 at Gloucester there were over 200 voices, and 301 performers all told from Lancashire, Yorkshire, Norwich, Oxford, Lichfield, Bristol and Birmingham. Now that more concerts were held in the cathedrals there was the problem of where to put them all and specially built platforms were erected in the nave. This problem became greater as the size of the orchestra gradually increased from a chamber group to one of symphonic proportions.

Fortunately for those who sing, Mendelssohn came along at the right time. His St. Paul (1837) and Hymn of Praise (1841) immediately became Festival favourites; more so than Beethoven's Mount of Olives (1842) and Mass in C (1847). Seen and heard now from a safe distance we can generalize sweepingly about Mendelssohn's music with its pleasant tunes and heart-on-sleeve youthful style of composition and suggest that it would have been much more easily assimilated by an audience that sought a morning of musical entertainment, than would Beethoven's brooding introspection. Experience tells us also that Mendelssohn's music is much easier to sing than Beethoven's, being without the dangers of unexpected bear pits, man traps and precipices waiting for us just over the page. Goodness knows how the chorus coped with Beethoven's music in 1842 when it was new!

Indeed there are accounts of performances which came to abrupt halts or dwindled into silence. One of these was later, in 1865, when Beethoven's Choral Fantasia under the direction of Wesley came to pieces. According to the critic of the *Morning Herald* 'the chorus was too big and didn't know their parts; the conductor couldn't take his eyes off the score to call them together.' Wesley was known as an organist and composer but not as a choir master. He habitually left the training of the choristers to one of the lay clerks.

Even Mendelssohn's works had the occasional unsatisfactory rendition, due perhaps to the wayward conducting technique of some of the cathedral organists. In previous times, an orchestra, or 'band' of some dozen or so instrumentalists and a choir of 40 would have been directed by the leader or concert master. This was fine for Purcell, Boyce and Handel, but given more complicated instrumentation and a choir of 200, suddenly there was a need for a leader who could give undivided attention to the forces in front of him, without having to play the violin at the same time. He must also be able to beat time reliably and see to chorus entries and dynamics. It was no longer possible for the first violinist to do all this and understandably the cathedral organists were sometimes out of their depth. The escalating problem of new music being in an unfamiliar idiom, added to a system of chorus rehearsal which gave them only one day to become acclimatized to the sound of the orchestral parts, the acoustic of the building, the eccentricities of the local organist, the entries of soloists, and the feeling of singing in a huge choir. Here was a recipe for disaster, which quite often occurred. One hundred years earlier, when everything was on a smaller scale, the Monday set aside for rehearsal was adequate, particularly as all the singers had sung the pieces somewhere else already and, arriving with soloists and orchestra whom they knew, they came as a unit. Towards the 1850s there was a major change in the style of musical composition and a much higher expectation of the performers.

The Three Choirs Festival was not the only venue where the new choral works could be heard. The Birmingham Festival began in 1768 as a fundraiser for the General Hospital and by 1800 had become a triennial event. At one time there was considerable rivalry between the two Festivals and not a little looking-down-the-nose by the industrially revolutionized city at its country cousins. Some of the criticisms may have been justified, but to suggest that 'the good folks of Worcester are leagues in the rear of the general improvement of musical taste ... They are mere Goths, for instance, compared with their Birmingham neighbours', is ungenerous to say the least. The same critic (*The Musical World*) came to Hereford in 1837 and passed further judgement. 'The effect of chorus and orchestra appeared to be almost poverty-striken after having emerged from the great volumes of sound that had been ringing in our ears in Birmingham ... Hereford in itself is not of sufficient importance to uphold a Festival on a grand scale.' Perhaps it was true of the particular moment, or perhaps he had cloth ears and was insensitive to the atmosphere of a cathedral; and anyway, what happened to the Birmingham Festival?

But a little competition is not a bad thing and any publicity is good, Indeed, the musical public was soon seeking out other cities where large scale concerts could be attended. Liverpool, Leeds and Norwich soon had their own festivals, with many of the same visiting bands of singers and players continuing the pattern started long before.

1847 saw another great landmark in choral history with the arrival of Mendelssohn's Elijah in Gloucester. Performed in Birmingham the year before, this work was an instant success and fortunately *The Musical World* now had a new critic who journeyed to Gloucester from Paris especially to attend the performance. 'I have just listened to Elijah, the greatest masterpiece of modern music - and exceedingly well rendered. The sensation justified all that the Gloucester amateurs anticipated.' *The Times* reported that 'The performance was very far superior to what had been expected. The choruses have seldom been heard to go better ... an honour to all concerned producing entire satisfaction among the audience.'

From 1848, local amateur musicians were sometimes given the chance to join the chorus and the orchestra, and as the expense of bringing a contingent of up to 50 singers from Leeds was thought to be too much for the Festival stewards to bear, the opportunities became more frequent until in 1892 at Gloucester, 1897 at Hereford, and 1902 at Worcester the Festival Chorus was made up entirely from singers chosen from the Choral Societies of the three cities.

10 Choral Conglomerate

Hell is full of musical amateurs: music is the brandy of the damned.

From *Man and Superman* by George Bernard Shaw

Conglomerate may not be a word often used to describe a choir, but it seems appropriate. The singers are gathered together into a united mass without losing personal individuality.[1]

1843 (H) *Hereford Journal*. 'Errors can arise in the best of circles. At the start of "For unto us a child is born", Mr. Smith led off beating four quavers instead of four crotchets in the bar. Had the basses been watching the conductor they would have come in nine bars too soon.' However, as they weren't, disaster was avoided. This was a lucky escape by choir and conductor alike but doesn't condone non-attendance to the baton. The angels may have been watching over the performers on that occasion but most conductors should be watched like hawks.

1845 (W) The arrangement of performers that year were as follows: 'in front were the solo voices, male and female; the conductor's chair was a step or two behind these; the chorus filled up the first eight or ten rows of benches - the ladies on the right and the gentlemen on the left, looking from the orchestra; ...'

In this year *The Musical Times* stresses the advantages of 'the cultivation of a good body of local choristers', and noted that 'very successful beginnings towards this desired result have been made in Gloucester, Hereford and Worcester.'

1848 (W) Mendelssohn's Elijah, Part I of Haydn's Creation, Beethoven's Mount of Olives, Messiah, part of Haydn's Seasons. 'The choral body was strong, being largely augmented by drafts from the newly formed choral societies of Worcester and Gloucester.'

1850 (G) Elijah, Creation, Parts I & II, a considerable portion of Beethoven's first Mass, Messiah. 'Elijah ... The choruses were grand and effective and the whole performance gave great satisfaction.'

From *The Times*: 'Mr. Done has been training his own people for two months previous to the Festival, in consequence of which the professionals from the Metropolis found the Worcesterians quite up to the mark.'

1851 (W) Elijah, a considerable portion of Handel's Samson, Spohr's Last Judgement, Messiah. 'The chorus, selected almost entirely from the provincial choirs and choral societies, [Hereford, Gloucester, Worcester, Birmingham, Bradford, Leeds, without extra lay-clerks] showed effective discipline. The performance of Elijah, on the second morning appears to have given great satisfaction, especially in the choruses, which were said to have been rendered in a manner that, in some points, might have furnished a lesson to the metropolitan choristers.'

1859 (G) Fees paid to members of the chorus ranged from £1 12s 6d for the two boys from Cheltenham to £5 for each singer from away. The choir was made up as follows: London Exeter Hall 30, Liverpool 24, Worcester 42, Gloucester 50, Cheltenham 21, Hereford 14, Winchester 1, Norwich 3, St Albans 1, Bristol 1, Oxford 1, Winchcomb 3, Manchester 1, Quedgley 1, Windsor 1, Chester 1, Salisbury 1, Newport 1. Reading rather like football results, this makes a total of 197 from 18 different places! No wonder the only combined rehearsal, taking the whole of Monday, was a nightmare. At this Festival the soloist, Clara Novello received a fee of £210

1861 (H) 'Elijah ... The choruses were heard with sustained interest and produced a marked impression at every instance.' 'Last Judgement ... The choral singing was more satisfactory than in Elijah.' 'Samson ... The choruses went gloriously. Nothing could be finer than the rendering of "Then round about the starry throne", except it were the still grander "Fixed in his everlasting seat".' Haydn's Seasons, Mozart's Requiem, 'Mendelssohn's Hymn of Praise ... The choruses were grand and effective.'

The Festival of the Three Choirs in Worcester Cathedral, 1866

1862 (G) Of Elijah *The Times* reported: 'We are inclined to believe that music sounds better in Gloucester Cathedral than in any other sacred building where we have heard the experiment tried. ... in the nave and aisles, even behind the orchestra, it can be heard to perfection ... the bursts of harmony in the full choruses with full orchestral accompaniment vibrate through its length and breadth with indescribable grandeur; and such reverberation as there is ... adds rather a peculiar solemnity to the general effect that robs it of its clearness and precision. This was frequently noticed to-day in the choruses of Elijah - as, for example, the invocations of the Baalite priests, "Baal we cry to thee", etc. It may be added that, on the whole, while, to the credit of Mr. Amott, the times [tempi] were almost everywhere unimpeachable, just as they were at the Leeds Festival in 1858, but as they by no means invariably are elsewhere. Nor was the delicacy found wanting, except in very rare instances. In short by this performance Gloucester has fairly won Laurels.'

Of Mendelssohn's Hymn of Praise the same writer goes into further rhapsodic eulogies. This somewhat florid style of reporting makes more entertaining reading than the matter-of-fact accounts of previous years. Three of the oratorios at this Festival, Elijah, Hymn of Praise and Messiah were given with no combined rehearsal, thereby giving proof of the important assistance given by the local choral societies who had been rehearsing well before the Festival, but is not something of which the management should have been proud.

The chorus for this Festival numbered 202 and was made up of singers from Gloucester, Hereford, Worcester, Manchester, and Liverpool with cathedral lay clerks or singers from Dublin, Bristol and a bass from Winchcomb. The top soloist, Madame Tietjens received a fee of £367.

1867 (H) Last Judgement, Elijah, Israel in Egypt, Ruth, Messiah. '... the grand double choruses in Israel were sung with great precision ... The band and choruses performed their parts in Elijah admirably.' Of Ruth by Goldschmidt, 'Out of the many choruses which Ruth contains not one was gone through from end to end without impediment.' How refreshing to have an opinion uncluttered by cloying compliments and an honest account of a disaster!

1868 (G) An unfortunate misunderstanding between the orchestra and the conductor (Wesley) over the tempo at the beginning of Beethoven's Mass in C led to hopeless confusion throughout the Kyrie so that the movement came to a sudden collapse and was recommenced. In contrast, however, the final

Principal Vocalists.

MDME. LIND GOLDSCHMIDT, MISS EDITH WYNNE,
AND
MADEMOISELLE TIETJENS.

MISS JULIA ELTON, & MADAME PATEY WHYTOCK.

| MR SIMS REEVES, & | MR. SANTLEY, & |
| MR. MONTEM SMITH, | MR. WEISS. |

Organ - - - Mr. DONE.   Pianoforte - - Dr. WESLEY.

CONDUCTOR - - MR. G. TOWNSHEND SMITH.

The Instrumental Band.

Violins :
MR H. BLAGROVE, Principal.   Mr. J. T. WILLY, Principal Second.
MESSRS. BARTHOLOMEW, CARRODUS, CLEMENTI, COLCHESTER, DANDO, DAY GOODWIN, H. W. HILL, H. HOLMES, E. S. JONES, RENDLE, THIRLWALL, THOMAS, WATSON, WOODWARD, ZERBINI, ZERBINI, JUN., ETC.

Violas :
Mr. R. BLAGROVE, Principal,   Mr. GLANVILLE, Principal Second.
MESSRS. BROOKE, T. REYNOLDS, TRUST, WESLAKE, WHEELER, ETC.

Violoncellos :
Mr G COLLINS, Principal   Mr. H. CHIPP, Principal Second.
MESSRS. G. CALKIN, CHAMPION DAUBERT, PETTIT, REED, WAITE.

Double Basses.
MR HOWELL, Principal.   Mr. SEVERN, Principal Second.
MESSRS BURVILL, EDGAR, C. HARPER, JUN., A. JONES, REYNOLDS, WHITE.

| Flutes : | Harp : | Oboes : |
| MESSRS. PRATTEN, E. CARD. | MR. TRUST. | MESSRS. NICHOLSON, G. HORTON. |

Clarionets :
MESSRS. LAZARUS, TYLER.

| Bassoons : | Trumpets : |
| MESSRS. WAETZIG, ANDERSON. | MESSRS. T. HARPER, WARD. |

Horns :
MESSRS. C. HARPER, MANN, CATCHPOLE, STANDEN.

Trombones :
MESSRS. HAWKES, HORTON, HEALEY, JUN.

| Euphonium : | Drums : | Side-Drum : |
| MR. PHASEY. | MR. F. HORTON. | MASTER GOODWIN. |

The CHORAL BAND will be considerably larger than in 1864, and is selected from the three Cathedral Choirs, Bristol, &c., the Choral Societies of Hereford, Gloucester, Worcester, Bradford, London, Oxford, &c.

AN ORGAN WILL BE ERECTED BY MR. NICHOLSON.

LIBRARIAN - - - - - - - - - - - MR. W. GOODWIN.

A page from the 1867 programme showing the composition of the chorus (note the part in italics near the foot of the page) attraction of the Festival was Messiah and the complete success of the band and chorus under Dr. Wesley's baton produced the customary imposing and thrilling effects.

1871 (G) Bach's St Matthew Passion was included in the Festival for the first time. Sadly the work was under-rehearsed, badly conducted and at one point broke down completely. On this day the cathedral programme began at 11.30a.m. and finished at 5p.m. The audience dwindled as the day wore on.

1874 (G) Chorus expenses £780, and the fee received by Madame Tietjens was £350.

1875 (W) No Festival occurred due to objections raised by the Dean and Chapter as to the matter of admittance to the cathedral by payment, the irrev- erence shown in the House of God, and the preparation of staging causing interruptions in daily services. There was therefore a Choral Festival of the three cathedral choirs only, without orchestra and soloists, giving a series of anthems with organ accompaniment.

1876 (H) Happily, the Dean and Chapter of Hereford did not share the same views. Bradford furnished a contingent of 40 voices and the following extract from one of the leading newspapers shows the estimation in which it was held:
'These ladies and gentlemen deserve special mention for their services which have been of the most valuable character throughout. Their finished and solid vocalization has been of the very greatest service in the oratorios, and in the evening concerts the selection they have performed have been amongst the most pleasing in the programme.'

1877 (G) Elijah, Bach's St Matthew Passion, Beethoven's Mount of Olives, Brahms' German Requiem, Mendelssohn's Hymn of Praise, Messiah. 'The chorus was supplied by the three cities, with contingents from London, Oxford, Cambridge, Wells, Bristol, Birmingham, Leicester, Manchester and Huddersfield.' The chorus expenses amounted to £826.

1878 (W) The Festival was at least permitted but no platform was provided, resulting in the singers and orchestra being at ground level in front of the choir screen.

1879 (H) Parts I & II of Bach's Christmas Oratorio received their first performance at the Festival.

1880 (G) 'Parry's Prometheus Unbound met with a distinctly mixed reception. The work was rehearsed inadequately from parts full of mistakes; the performance, in the over-loaded type of programme then usual, and with a tired band and chorus, in a poor light, was saved from disastrous inadequacy partly by the generous action of the Huddersfield contingent of the chorus, which, unknown to Parry, met for a special extra rehearsal on the very day of the concert.'

1881 (W) Elijah, The Creation parts I & II, Beethoven's Mount of Olives, Cherubini's Mass in D, Messiah. 'Monday was, as usual given up to rehearsals from 9.45 a.m. to 11 p.m., when band, chorus and soloists retired to their well-earned and much-needed rest. It was generally admitted on all sides that more rehearsals were needed, one day being totally inadequate for rehearsing more than a quarter of the week's work.' A platform was erected at the West end and the audience's seats ran east to west so that their backs were not turned to the altar.

1882 (H) 'Elijah ... An excellent performance was secured by Mr Colborne.' Bach's Magnificat, Mendelssohn's St Paul, Beethoven's Choral Fantasia, Messiah. (Programmes are becoming well filled by the heavyweights of choral music.)
    'A contingent of 52 voices was selected from the [Bradford] society to take part in the Hereford Musical Festival of 1882. This engagement was fulfilled to the entire satisfaction of Mr. Langdon Colborne, the talented conductor, and of the Festival Committee. On this occasion two of the choral works were allotted safely to the Bradford contingent; it was also called upon to sing no less than seven madrigals and part-songs - an amount of work without precedent at any previous festival. The President of the Society, Mr. Averdieck, who accompanied the party, presented each member of the contingent with a photograph of the whole body!'[2]

1883 (G) 'A contingent of 20 voices [from the Bradford society] was for the first time, furnished for the Gloucester Musical Festival and Mr. Lee Williams, the organist and conductor of the Festival, expressed great satisfaction with the manner in which the contingent fulfilled its duties on the occasion.'[3]

1884 (W) Dvorak's Stabat Mater, Cherubini's Mass in D minor, Elijah, Messiah. 'The singing of the chorus came in for an unusual share of censure at this Festival, the chief cause of complaint being that the parts were unevenly balanced. Monday was taken up by rehearsals all day.'

1885 (H) Elijah, Stabat Mater, Gounod's Redemption, Last Judgement, Hymn of Praise, Messiah. Monday as usual was devoted to incessant rehearsals from morning till night. Only those who have had to act in the responsible position of conductor at these Festivals can adequately appreciate the great mental anxiety (and inevitable failure) of trying to rehearse a week's work in one day. Many things, of course, are left entirely unrehearsed and have to take their chance, especially when Festival programmes teem with new works of all kinds that must be gone through with care (and generally at great length). Considering all the disadvantages, it seems wonderful how well the unre-hearsed parts of the Festival programme seem to go; possibly the proverbial pluck of our national character comes out when all concerned are perfectly aware of their situation. The Bradford contingent of the chorus sang an eight-part song called "Twilight" by Mr. Lee Williams, with excellent effect.'
    'In this year also [1885] a contingent of 40 voices was furnished for the Hereford Musical Festival, this being one of the long established "Three Choirs" Festivals of the cathedrals of Worcester, Hereford and Gloucester.'[4]

1886 (G) The chorus was supplied by singers from the following towns: Worcester 37, (including lay-clerks and 4 boys), Tewkesbury 9, Cardiff 20, Bradford 24, Gloucester Festival Class 60, (including lay-clerks and boys), Bristol 20, Hereford 29 (including 8 lay-clerks and 4 boys), Cambridge 4 lay-clerks, Oxford 8 lay-clerks. A total of 301. The Festival Class was for singers chosen from choral societies and church choirs throughout the county.

1887 (W) Elijah, Schubert's Mass in E flat, Last Judgement, Cowen's Ruth, Messiah. 'At a performance in the Public Hall of Sullivan's "Golden Legend" the chorus was composed entirely of the Leeds contingent of the Festival Choir, and their rendering of the choruses is acknowledged to have been a very pattern of what chorus-singing should be.'

1888 (H) The Golden Legend, Elijah, Samson, Creation parts I & II, Cherubini's Mass in D minor, Parry's Blest Pair of Sirens, Messiah. 'The chorus which, owing to limited space was small, consisted of 100 local singers [i.e. from Hereford, Gloucester and Worcester] with 50 members of the Leeds choir', of whom the Daily News wrote, 'that there was no difficulty in recognising the Leeds voices, and particularly the ringing brightness of the sopranos and the deep sonority of the basses.' A group such as this would have been rehearsed at home but the actual chorus at concerts would have been built up of so many fragments that break-down was almost inevitable.

1889 (G) The organist of Gloucester, Lee Williams, wrote in his little black book 'Extra day put on in London at my urgent request. Quite impossible to do with less - even with two days, more than half the programme was performed without any rehearsal at all.' The committee was told that 'the chorus was, relatively, [to what, I wonder] the most expensive in the kingdom, inasmuch as its 200 voices cost £800. There were means by which this expense could be lessened, and Mr.Williams should be prepared to lay before the committee a scheme which, without impairing its efficiency, would lower the cost by £300.'

1890 (W) St. Paul, Creation, Mozart's Requiem, Parry's Ode to St Cecilia, written for the Leeds Festival, Dr. Bridge's 'Repentance of Nineveh ... The chorus and band ... acquitted themselves admirably. The invisible choir who were placed beneath the orchestra sang under difficulties, and became painfully flat.' 'Beethoven's Mount of Olives ... The performance was by no means fault-less, the conductor being compelled to beat the actual desk, as well as the metaphorical time ... The chorus ... was supplied by the three cathedral cities, with a contingent from Cardiff, as well as 80 ladies and gentlemen from Leeds.'

1891 (H) The choir was supplied by Hereford, Gloucester, Worcester, Oxford, with the Leeds contingent, who contributed two part-songs by Sullivan and Mackenzie at the Secular Concert.

Some programmes were extremely long. A morning concert of Mozart's Requiem, Stainer's St. Mary Magdalen, Mendelssohn's Hymn of Praise, Lloyd's Song of Judgement, Parry's De Profundis - 130th Psalm, a Bach Motet for double chorus and quartet sung unaccompanied, Mackenzie's Benedictus, Spohr's Calvary, surely lasted well into the afternoon, leaving barely enough time for dinner before the performance of Elijah, yet another choral heavyweight.

Traditionally the final morning was reserved for Messiah. 'The band and chorus were thoroughly in their element.'

1892 (G) 'For the first time the resources of the counties of Hereford, Gloucester and Worcester were relied upon, and the help, up to that time thought necessary from Leeds, Bradford, Cardiff, and the chapels of Oxford and Cambridge, dispensed with. The result was that the chorus, on this occasion, proved itself more than equal to every requirement and abundantly justified the great experiment. The opinion generally expressed was that in attack, phrasing and expression, the chorus of the Three Choirs in 1892 - minus the expensive help from foreign sources compared favourably with any similar body at Festivals of either of the Three Choirs for many previous years.' *The Musical Times* said 'It was a capital body of singers, fit for anything.'

Of Elijah, 'As regards the chorus the parts were excellently balanced, the tone was good, the attack prompt and correct.' Gounod's Redemption, Handel's Joshua, 'The chorus showed throughout that they were equal to the varied styles of singing.' Dr. Bridge's Lord's Prayer, Lee Williams Gethsemane, 'Bach's cantata ... My spirit was in heaviness ... An extremely difficult work, and it must be confessed that neither principals nor chorus came quite successfully out of the trying ordeal.' Parry's Job. Spohr's Fall of Babylon, 'Mendelssohn's Hymn of Praise ... The chorus, though they had a very hard day again covered themselves in glory, singing the difficult and exacting numbers as freshly and as vigorously as at any time during the week.' And on Friday, Messiah.

1893 (W) 'It was hoped that Worcester ... would follow the excellent lead set by Gloucester ... and dispense with other voices than those supplied by the three counties; but Worcester decided to walk in the old ways and Mr. Broughton's Leeds Choir of a hundred voices formed half the chorus.' This continued dependence upon these highly trained singers from the north was a source of shame and embarrassment to Worcester Choral Society, as was the fact that very few of their members were invited to go to Hereford and Gloucester. A Festival visitor wrote to *The Times* as follows;-

'Three Choirs Festival
Pray allow me to protest as publicly as possible against the further use of the above title at this festival. Out of a chorus of 200 voices (more or less) I observe the astounding statement that

a large contingent - *viz.* nearly 100 voices - has been imported from Leeds. In these days of advanced musical knowledge, and with colleges and schools of music as plentiful as blackberries, do the authorities really mean to assert that in the combined counties of Worcester, Gloucester and Hereford 200 competent singers cannot be found to sing the very ordinary programme that the committee offer for performance this week? ... Musical readers may recollect that at Gloucester last year the committee resolved, apart from the voices very properly contributed by Hereford and Worcester, to find their chorus exclusively within the boundaries of the county. They made the experiment and were not disappointed. The Gloucestershire singers, with a comparatively small number of allies from the sister shires, answered all requirements, and so was removed a long-standing provocation to criticism. I am told that some sort of agreement was come to among the organists of the three cathedrals with a view to make the festival dioceses sufficient unto themselves in the manner of chorus-singers, but this, if it ever existed, could not bind the committee, and the Worcester managers have here a hundred voices from Leeds ... it may be of interest to state that Gloucestershire has just formally united its vocal resources for festival purposes. A meeting of representatives of choral societies within the county was held last week, under the presidency of Mr. C. Lee Williams, with the result that festival performances may henceforth be organized anywhere within the shire in full assurance of a competent chorus ... The example of its sister county is worth, at any rate, the serious consideration of Worcestershire.'

It is heart-warming to find such an ardent and voluble supporter of the home teams of the 1890s but a little amusing to discover that in the particular year in which Gloucester advocated Independence, Bristol sent 100 singers as members of the Gloucester Choral Society! Maybe Bristol wasn't in Somerset that year, or perhaps these 100 were 'affiliated'. No matter, at least they didn't have to travel 200 miles.

Elijah, Israel in Egypt, 'Bach's Mass in B minor ... a truly splendid performance ... the rendering of the majestic "Sanctus" by the chorus being especially fine.' Parry's Job, Brahms' German Requiem, Messiah.

1894 (H) The chorus was supplied by Hereford, Gloucester, Worcester and Leeds. At the Secular Concert, Hereford Festival Class provided the chorus for a new work by Lloyd, 'The ballad of Sir Ogie and the Lady Elsie'. Dvorak's Requiem, Bridge's 'The Cradle of Christ', Bach's Christmas Oratorio, Parts I & II of The Creation, Mackenzie's Bethlehem, Spohr's Last Judgement, Parry's Job, Mendelssohn's Hymn of Praise, Messiah.

1895 (G) Cowen's The Transfiguration. Brahms' Song of Destiny.

1896 (W) Elgar's Light of Life. Verdi's Requiem. The organist in charge was Hugh Blair, a close friend of Edward Elgar from the days when he led the Festival orchestra. Blair was ambitious in programme planning, putting forward the first performance of Elgar's Light of Life and Verdi's Requiem, but had difficulty in preparing the troops for battle. Maybe he couldn't settle down to the concentrated hard grind of weekly rehearsals now needed by contemporary music.

Another letter, this time to the *Birmingham Daily Gazette*:

> 'Hereford 1896
> Sir, it is all very well to lament over the small number of engage-
> ments sent to the Worcester choristers when the festivals are held
> at Hereford and Gloucester. No persons are more anxious for the
> entire chorus to be drawn from the three counties than the author-
> ities in those two cities last named; but as one who may be
> allowed to speak on behalf of those authorities may I throw out
> a hint to our friends at Worcester? Some conductors do not
> consider that a few rehearsals of only 40 minutes duration are
> sufficient to prepare the Worcester contingent for the festivals
> held in Gloucester and Hereford, and until they are assured that
> the Worcester singers are well versed in the works to be
> produced, it is not surprising that the 'powers that be' at the two
> sister cities send so many engagements to the towns where 60
> rehearsals are not considered too much for a festival. We have
> had ample proof this week of what the three choirs are capable
> of, and it is a crying shame that such talent is not made the most
> of. - Yours, etc.'

11 Rehearsal

I hear a gay modulating anguish, rather like music.
From 'The lady's not for burning' by Christopher Fry

The Oxford English Dictionary gives the definition of to rehearse as 'to rake over', derived from the Middle English, 'hearse' or 'herse', meaning a harrow, the same root as the coffin cart. I like the idea of raking over the notes until the imperfections are set aside, like the unwanted stones in my garden.

Think of a time before the days of the Royal College of Music, Young Musician of the Year and the Eurovision Song Contest. How did the young-ster with a compulsion to make music extend his knowledge? Before the age of hi-fi, multi track and C.D., how would he find out about different ways of playing the same piece?

It is quite a thought that until the 20th century, most people's experience of listening to music other than that made at home, was in church, on the village green on Fair Days, or very occasionally in a concert hall. Even until the mid-20th century, this was only extended to the wind-up gramophone and radio. The chance offered by the local choral society to partake in public music-making was taken up by many because, in being part of a concert performance one was allowed to stand shoulder to shoulder with the profes-sional musician and learn even more. The hobby of singing opened doors into the world of creativity.

Although these pages are angled at the happenings at the Three Choirs Festival, it is nevertheless to the north once again that we turn. Oldham, repre-senting Lancashire; Leeds, Huddersfield, Wakefield, York and Bradford all in Yorkshire; were not merely hot-spots of musical activity, they were glowing furnaces, burning with the white heat of enthusiasm and set on the mainstream of excellence. The great choral societies of these towns were the social life of many and to become a member was the ambition of a large number of singers. Rules and regulations about membership were tough—no absenteeism, no alcohol, no lewd language!

Here was a fine opportunity for the 'Education of the Working Class' as well as for the furthering of their enjoyment of music, and the enlightened leaders of a town, be they mill owners or churchmen, were well aware of the possibilities offered through musical education. More than one mill and factory had its own school, brass band and choral union, thus keeping the populace off the streets and out of the ale-houses while offering them a chance to improve the mind.

Activities which took place after work hours were more accessible to men than to women. In 1837 the Huddersfield Choral Society had 62 performing members of whom only eight were ladies. Men took the Bass, Tenor and Alto parts and some of them even managed the Soprano line, though the very thought brings tears to the eyes.

This was the year of Queen Victoria's accession. It was also the time of full employment for women in factories at least until they married and transferred their energy to home and countless children. Not many of them were able to go out and sing, either because they were working until nightfall or because it was not thought proper for a married woman to be out without her husband, nor for an unmarried one to be unchaperoned. Fortunately, musical societies have always provided a meeting ground for courting couples, and in an age when 'respectability' was of paramount importance, the choral society, having connections with sacred music and the church organist, a man employed by the church and therefore assumed to be above suspicion, was deemed safe enough for young girls to attend.

Rivalries between Choral Societies in the northern towns grew in intensity as musical competence increased and repertoires widened. Here fiercely partisan fires were being fuelled by the spirit of the competitive music festival, something resembling the eisteddfodau of Wales. Choruses became bigger and bigger, music was chosen for its difficulty, to be a challenge and to show off the virtuosity of the singers, rules of membership became even more stringent and the audition was implemented. Rehearsals became weekly events and were solely for the purpose of perfecting the rendering of the notes. The age of innocent discovery of the art had been set aside.

Some time later, a provincial musician from a working class background attended Morecombe's competitive music festival and was greatly impressed by the standard of musicianship of the choirs. Edward Elgar, by 1904 well acquainted with London musical life, wrote to the organizer of the festival as follows:

> 'It is rather a shock to find Brahms' part-songs appreciated and among the daily fare of a district apparently unknown to the sleepy London press: people who talk of the spread of music in England and the increasing love of it, rarely seem to know where the growth of the art is really strong and properly fostered. Some day the press will awake to the fact, already known abroad and to some few of us in England, that the living centre of music in Great Britain is not London, but somewhere further north.'

Confusingly, besides the eisteddfod type of festival, often held at the seaside so that competitors could go on the train for a day out, each town also had its own Music Festival of the non-competitive variety, and for this the same familiar programmes were repeated year after year and in every town—Messiah, Elijah, Spohr's Last Judgement, madrigals and glees. Such was the high standard of performance that, first Bradford in 1858, then The Yorkshire Choral Union, an amalgam of 200 voices from Halifax, Leeds and Huddersfield in 1860, were commanded to sing at Buckingham Palace before Queen Victoria, and subsequently at Crystal Palace before an immense audience of commoners. All these choralists must have been used to travelling great distances to their concert engagements, rather like their predecessors in the 18th century, but now in droves big enough to fill a train, unlike the five or six who went by stage-coach in 1772. For some reason, probably tradition (the adage 'its always been done like that', comes to mind), northern singers had continued to arrive in London in their hundreds to sing at the Great Exhibition and for the Handel Festivals. Presumably by the same reasoning they continued to come to the Three Choirs Festival even up to the 1890s, although well before then there were thriving choral societies in Hereford, Gloucester and Worcester—as there were everywhere else by mid-century. If their travelling expenses hadn't become too much of a financial burden, they might be coming still. However, although the style of singing and the tone of voice in middle western England didn't match that of our northern friends, the local choirs were, by the end of the century, quite as competent in producing the notes. So the Three Choirs Festival finally bade farewell to the spinners and weavers, the Deborahs and Williams, Sarahs and Ellens, the Radcliffe and Russell families, the mill girls, the women who sang as they worked at the loom and their men-folk, and became accustomed to a different sound, a chorus chosen by cathedral organists on their home ground, whose voices would blend with those of the boy choristers and the lay clerks of the cathedral choirs.

The small chorus of the 18th century had been a group of potential soloists, with some of the vocal power and personality that solo singers carry with them if they are to make an impression. The huge choruses of the 19th century were able to come up with the dynamic contrasts demanded by the music of the Romantic Period—Mendelssohn, Beethoven and Berlioz—but they were an unwieldy body, difficult for the conductor to shape and if anything went amiss, as it sometimes did, the disaster was the more noticeable.

There are countless parables, proverbs and sayings about sheep and I see no reason for excluding them from the choral scene. Like sheep, a large flock of singers is fine as long as they move along together, but, having gone astray, they become hopelessly lost, frightened and unpredictable, and make a dreadful noise!

12 Victoriana

Music, when soft voices die, vibrates in the memory.

Percy Bysshe Shelley

To many of us, the Victorian age means large families, ballads, potted ferns, lace curtains, the music-hall, and respectability. Alongside this romantic cameo came the reality of factory employment for millions, railway travel for thousands, and a puritanical attitude to legs which insisted on their being hidden; a quaint notion that even led to furniture being covered down to the floor lest the sight of the table legs corrupt the thoughts. This veneer of respectability in the home was one way in which society ignored the shame of much worse things than bare legs. In the towns it was back to back houses, poor sewerage, severe drunkenness, starvation, cholera and the workhouse. Poverty threatened everybody and needed to be faced. An ostrich mentality prevailed in many circles because there was just too much to be done, but the gulf between rich and poor which had not become any narrower than in the previous century was at last being talked about in parliament, its presence was being questioned by both sides and reforms were gradually being made in the areas of education and health.

The life-styles of mill workers of the north could not have been more different from that of the predominantly farming community of the three counties. In Yorkshire and Lancashire the energy that went into mining coal, digging canals and setting up factories to produce more and better cloth was reflected in a demand for education among the workers and an enthusiasm for the kind of social activity that also involved learning and thinking. Choral singing and the brass band movement became synonymous with the northern factories and coal mines—as they did in a slightly different way a little later in the Welsh valleys.

The Industrial Revolution had had a less traumatic effect on the three cities of Hereford, Gloucester & Worcester although from 1772 onwards canals had been built with the intention of linking them commercially with the great network of inland waterways and from 1830 onwards railways made them accessible to all and sundry.

Here, choral singing came by a different route. Great Aunt Agatha was something of a singer. She had graduated from the Methodist Chapel choir to the local choral society where she sang soprano. At that time the alto line was sung mostly by men; there were far more men than women in the society because a young woman would be unable to continue her membership when family duties demanded her full attention. She met John, her future husband, at choir meetings. He sang in the bass section and, being quite a few years older than she, had more experience of the music and took it upon himself to help the new member. One thing led to another and soon they were 'walking out' on their days off.

Agatha was employed as a seamstress by a dressmaker in the town and worked very long hours in a room full of girls making clothes for the gentry of Gloucestershire. It was pleasant enough to be working with her friends but she enjoyed choir evenings all the more for their being such a change and for the company being a bit more educated. John had been apprenticed to a carpenter and cabinet maker so was a skilled worker. This set him up a notch in the social scale. At the end of his seven years he went into partnership with a piano maker. Every household now had to have a piano in the parlour and there was a constant demand for tuning, repair or a new instrument. Much of their courtship was spent learning music together and when Agatha's father bought a piano, their happiness knew no bounds since now they could go into the parlour, unchaperoned, with the valid excuse of 'having to go through our parts'. John was an accomplished pianist as well as a singer and soon after they married he was asked to be the accompanist, then conductor of the town's Choral Society. He saw this post as a great honour and worked hard to teach the singers their notes by whatever method he and they found to be effective.

On the occasion of his 25 years as conductor he was presented with a silver and ebony baton lying in a silk-lined morocco leather case. This was a very grand piece, not to be used, of course, but to be placed for all to see in the

Rehearsal of Three Choirs chorus with Sinclair at Hereford in September 1900. The great west window was being repaired— hence the sheeting behind the chorus

glass cupboard. Agatha remembered the happy times they all had together in the choral society—the picnics, when the whole chorus went by train to the seaside for the day; the competitive festivals, for which they rehearsed night after night until they were note perfect; and the Three Choirs Festivals when people from small choral societies like theirs, were joined together in a Chorus of 200 voices in the cathedral and had to learn such a lot of music. She remembered particularly the difficulties of new pieces like Sullivan's Golden Legend; Parry's Job; Mendelssohn's Hymn of Praise and St. Paul; Dvorak's Stabat Mater and Requiem Mass; The Light of Life by Mr. Elgar, a young man from Worcester; Brahms' Requiem and Song of Destiny; the relief of reaching the Messiah concert and the favourite work of everybody, Mendelssohn's Elijah with that marvellous chorus 'Baal we cry to thee' which always came over as 'Bill we cry to thee' much to Uncle William's amusement.

In those days the men dressed up very smartly in black suits with wing collars and a black tie. Ladies wore white dresses and, because they were singing in the house of God, their costume had to include a hat. Agatha wasn't very tall and there were many times when she couldn't see Mr. Williams, the conductor because of the heap of flowers, feathers and netting on the head of the lady in front. Some hats were quite ridiculously out of keeping, being more of a fancy-dress than a garment suitable for singing Elijah, and at some point a suggestion was made that the ladies of the chorus should 'modify their headwear to a discreet and less intrusive covering'. Agatha remembered well one year when September was unusually hot, dresses had very high collars and waists were nipped in by tight whalebone corsets and two ladies had to be revived with smelling salts when they were overcome by the heat and having to stand for such a long time. Really it was a wonder there were not more cases of fainting on that platform.

Her sisters, Mary and Emily, sometimes attended the concerts in the Shirehall but they didn't sing in the Festival. Mary always claimed that her voice sounded like a donkey braying so she didn't even go for a voice trial, but limited her musical performances to Mendelssohn's 'Songs without Words' on the piano. Emily tried, but her singing was more like a sparrow than a nightingale and Mr. Williams wanted ladies who could sing a lot louder. Some of the new pieces, like the Requiem by Verdi, required enormous stamina and dear Em had always been a bit delicate.

Memories of Festival concerts mingled with recollections of the younger members of the church choir going off to a neighbouring chapel or hall for an evening of recitations and songs, always including in the programme, by special request, 'Come into the garden, Maud', Emily's favourite, and a chorus from Messiah. She still had the copy of Messiah that John had used when he conducted it.

In 1902, when two of Agatha's children were in the Chorus—Reginald in the tenors and Dorothy in the altos—there was sense of decorum and the young ladies were all kept under the eye of one of the older ladies, as well as the Chorus Superintendent. This was particularly necessary if they went away to one of the other two cities. Only a few singers would be asked to travel each year as the city whose turn it was to be host would provide the bulk of the chorus. Earlier in the year these chosen few were rehearsed in the music of the Festival by their own conductors, Mr. Sinclair in Hereford, Mr. Brewer in Gloucester and Mr. Atkins in Worcester, and the complete Festival Chorus met for a combined rehearsal in July before the summer holiday. Then there was a dangerously long time between this practice and the Festival in September. Much was forgotten or never learnt and the last minute panic on the Saturday before the Grand Opening Service was carried over to Monday. As in 1770 there were still no concerts on Mondays. Instead, in 1902, there was relentless rehearsing from 9.30 a.m. until 5.30 p.m. of all the music programmed for the next four days—or as much of it as it was possible to do. This punishing workload became known by the chorus as Black Monday, for after the first few hours no good could come of the exercise anyway and the result was complete exhaustion and confusion. It was a wonder that so many good performances did come about during the next four days. Elijah was always given on Tuesday morning and Messiah had its place on Friday morning, and these two works were so tried and trusted that no extra rehearsal time was given to them, but between these came new works by many up and coming young composers. Hubert Parry was still the chief composer for the Festival but he was joined by Walford Davies, Coleridge Taylor, Granville Bantock, Brewer and Edward Elgar. In a programme full of new music, there were, in that year, two mountains to overcome; Walford Davies' The Temple and Elgar's Dream of Gerontius.

During the months leading up to Festival week the three parts of the chorus, separated from each other by hills, valleys and 30 odd miles, worked hard to understand the complexity of The Dream and to do justice to the beauty of the music. They were used to the drama of Elijah, an oratorio which, like Handel's, could have been an opera had its theme not been a religious one, wherein Mendelssohn's orchestration mirrors the story and the hopes, fears and thankfulness of the characters become very real through the music. That story was already familiar from Bible study at church and Sunday School and the crowds asking Baal for rain were ordinary people living through a drought. Being asked to produce a chorus of demons, souls in purgatory and angelicals, placed greater demands on singers and posed a challenge to an audience brought up on the hymns of Sankey and Moody. There is indeed a hymn in Gerontius, but not a straightforward version and the whole work, being the story of the passage from life to death is a fantasy of massive proportions, touching on fear, delight, weariness, wonderment, regret and reassurance in a way which is not of this world. This, according to Elgar in a letter to his friend Jaeger, 'is not an oratorio. There's no word invented yet to describe it.'

Looking at the programmes of this period, it is evident that the 1902 debut in Worcester of The Dream of Gerontius projected Elgar to the elevated position held by Handel and Mendelssohn. A certain amount of bias is permitted since he was a local lad and the programme planners were determined that every one of his works should be performed during the Festivals. The

Apostles (1904) and The Kingdom (1907) are difficult works to learn. The train of thought behind the words is often broken for other interjections and the music is subject to mood swings which performer and listener have to travel with, not just follow. The chorus, now standing on its own three feet, without the help of extras, was certainly put on its mettle to do justice to Elgar's music and in the years 1905 - 1908 two of the three choral works were heard at each Festival, a huge undertaking which demonstrates, besides an immediate recognition of the greatness of the music, a wish to adopt the unmistakable idiom as The Three Choirs Sound. This surely was the time when Elgar was absorbed into the Chorus blood stream so completely that the singers of nearly a hundred years later still have it in their genes and chromosones. Given a copy of any Elgar work, familiar to them or not, they will find their way into it instinctively, causing the emergence of a beatific smile on a conductor's face and giving rise to the comment, 'You feel safe with this music, don't you.'

13 Wind of Change

The singing will never be done.
From 'Everyone Sang' by Siegfried Sassoon

When the link with Bradford, Leeds and Halifax, the three largest, loudest and strongest suppliers of voices, was broken after 120 years of continuity, there must have been tears on both sides. Friendships had been formed with land-ladies and householders who had taken in, fed and watered. The people who had formed the visiting contingents had made their own special friendships with each other after their days and nights of travelling and singing. Suddenly the counties north of the Mersey were estranged; too far away for a casual visit without the bond of the festival, they once again became as a foreign land, and the Meeting of the Three Choirs was in some danger of becoming just another provincial festival. Repercussions were both good and bad.

On the good side was local pride and much more personal involvement of home-grown talent, both in band and chorus. As far back as 1878 Edward Elgar, his father and his uncle were playing in the orchestra in Worcester, but singers had to wait another 20 years to claim a regular seat on the platform. With this wind of change, the triennial invasion of foreigners was a thing of the past. The choral conglomerations who came and lived in the place for a week, staying in lodging houses and regarding the cathedrals as beautiful big concert halls were seen no more. Now the people of the towns could contribute and take responsibility. Local singers who couldn't bear to go through the summer months without music could join the Festival Class of the Choral Society and rehearse the music over several weeks, and their friends and relations were encouraged to offer help in the myriad of humdrum tasks

91

that hold the festival together. This was indeed a huge step forward in the development of the Meetings.

On the downside, however, with the loss of the northern contingents went that special type of voice with an edged clarity, the Gracie Fields tone which the singer from the English mid-west doesn't have. Without this, the overall sound of the chorus changed and it must be admitted sometimes fell into a murkiness which the early recordings do not commend.

Another great loss was a contact with the big wide world outside Hereford, Gloucester and Worcester. From the very beginning there had been notices about the Meetings in national newspapers and the whole country would have known about its existence. It was, in the 18th century, a *National* Music Meeting. As early as 1750 when transport must have been quite hazardous, a singing man from Cambridge and another from Liverpool came to augment the choirs. In the 1830s, with the arrival of railways, crowds were able to come, but by 1900, when it had become possible to travel almost anywhere with ease and comfort, the cost became too high and the link was broken. Who in present-day Bradford can boast of a connection, who in Leeds has any record of a great grandmother or great grandfather singing Elijah in Worcester? Who in Halifax or Huddersfield has even heard of the Three Choirs Festival?

Perhaps this enforced change of gear, change of sound, attitude and apti-tude has, overall, been beneficial in hindsight. Things that don't develop tend to die out as did numerous Music Festivals in other places. This one is still in its youth and growing. The 20th century chorus has become an exceedingly determined band of musicians, still a happy mix of amateur and professional, still mostly anonymous, still sitting on hard wooden benches precariously erected and slung between the pillars in cathedrals which are still as awesome, beautiful, acoustically challenging and worthy of every-thing we can give as they were in 1715 or so. In the midst of such architec-ture we can appreciate the meaning of *Nobilmente*, one of Elgar's favourite musical instructions.

Edward Elgar was brought up in Worcester, in a musical family and in the shadow of the cathedral and its music—daily services, Three Choirs Meetings, processionals, organ music, and visiting players and singers—so it is no wonder he was able to write with such a sure feeling for the sound of a cathedral performance. Although written for the Birmingham Festivals, and first performed in the Town Hall there, The Dream of Gerontius, The

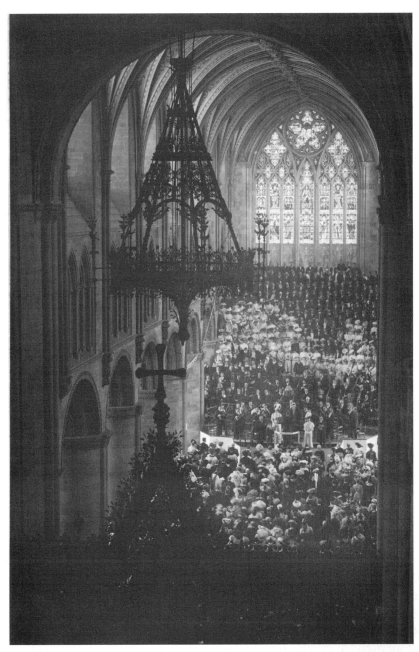

The Hereford Festival, 11th September 1906

Kingdom, and The Apostles fit the very fabric of the cathedral building as a glove fits a hand. To me the pillars, vaulted ceilings, demonic gargoyles and stained glass angels are an extension to the music. I have known performances in other places, albeit with faultless intonation and rhythmic excellence, which have yet lacked something spiritual. Bring that music back home to Worcester, Hereford or Gloucester and feel the empathy between performers and audience, the respect they hold for the composer and the love of his work.

In the Dream, the chorus 'Praise to the Holiest in the Height' reaches up to the pinnacles on the tower. Sopranos and Altos who only this morning were standing in the queue at Safeways are become winged and haloed angelicals; Basses and Tenors have no problem in taking on the guise of demons and join the effigies carved by stonemasons determined to frighten everyone away. Gerontius and his Angel sing a love duet far surpassing anything seen on the operatic stage. This music was written by a man whose musical education was gained from being born and brought up in Worcestershire and through playing in the orchestra at Three Choirs Meetings, and it shows.

Just at the time when it seemed the English musical scene was reaching new heights of excellence unknown in the previous century, and the new man, Vaughan Williams was adding yet another ingredient to the choral menu with his Five Mystical Songs, performed in 1911 at Worcester, and Fantasia on Christmas Carols, performed the following year at Hereford, the world came to one of mankind's periodic climaxes of intolerance and declared war upon itself. Such a totally useless occupation can only leave populations destitute, deranged or dead, and deny a generation a secure childhood, yet somehow and sometimes it makes room for philosophical sayings and heart stopping music.

The 1914 Worcester Festival was prepared but had to be cancelled and stored at the back of the organist's mind for six years. Had it not been for the persistence and strength of Ivor Atkins, who in 1920 fought against the doubts and delays of Worcester's cathedral authorities, the Festival might never have come out of hiding at all. Happily, the Worcester public were persuaded to revive a pre-war programme and it must have been a very emotional gathering of friends who heard yet again the familiar words and music of Messiah, Gerontius, Elijah, Hymn of Praise and Verdi Requiem. Elgar's For the Fallen and The Music Makers had their first performance at this Festival. How could it *not* take place?

Dona Nobis Pacem

> Everyone suddenly burst out singing.
>
> From 'Everyone Sang' by Siegfried Sassoon

It takes more than a world war to stop the singing and once the mighty wheels were turning again, energy was generated to produce bigger and better Festivals, even if some of the orchestral players hadn't come home from the battlefields. Maybe it was a more solemn and reverent gathering of people, maybe some of the parties had been cut short, maybe fashion was not so extravagant, nevertheless, in 1921, Percy Hull, himself a victim of the evil of war and newly come to Hereford, managed a most successful debut with the inclusion of Holst's Hymn of Jesus. Remarked upon at the time as 'being a recent work of great novelty and difficulty', it hasn't become any easier, but fairly regular performances have given it the chance to become part of our choral heritage. Mr. Hull was greatly helped at this his first Festival, by Elgar and W.H. Read. In The Apostles the semi-chorus were nine male voices, representing the Apostles, for the first time in accordance with the composer's instructions.

1922 at Gloucester heard Elijah, The Apostles, The Kingdom, Messiah and Verdi's Requiem, and a wonderful experience it was, but Herbert Brewer, the Gloucester organist was looking around for more new works and found Bantock's Song of Songs and Goosens' Silence Poem, each conducted by their composers. The Goosens work set a new tradition of the chorus copy not being ready until the last minute, and Silence threatening to be all too realistic. The muse doesn't always visit when invited and maybe a composer cannot meet a deadline, neither can a printer always decipher the manuscript. The chorus received copies only a fortnight before the Festival and agreed to a daily rehearsal to become acquainted with the unfamiliar chromatic idiom. Even so they had difficulty in arriving at a unison B flat at the end, so Brewer installed a harmonium at the back of the platform to sound the note. Unfortunately the success of this plan was ruined by the deep rattling boom from a ciphering organ pipe.

As the Festival picked itself up again, a chorus had to be found. (Surely this would have proved impossible had it still travelled mostly from Bradford). Local church choirs and Choral Societies provided the backbone of the Festival Chorus, as they do to this day and there are still memories of a message coming from the cathedral organist asking for tenors and basses to go for an audition, and of one 20 year old singer being confronted with Messiah, Gerontius and Elijah for the first time and having to 'get on with it'. This particular gentleman remembers Zoltan Kodaly, Edward Elgar and Gustav Holst conducting their own music at the Festivals. As he says, 'we all took it for granted at that age, ... didn't realize how important these people were.'

Somewhere along the line the glees and madrigals were laid to rest and the Miscellaneous Concert, which had been a much loved and highly educational musical jumble sale in the 19th century, became a selection of small orchestral pieces or chamber works without the prima donna kind of soloist stealing the show. Maybe the loss of the Bradford contingent who excelled at glees and madrigals caused this change in programme making, maybe there was so much else for the chorus to do in cathedral concerts, maybe it was a change of fashion. In the 18th century these songs were extremely popular and were the entertainment of the very first Music Clubs, from which our Festival was born. They became the bread and butter of the new choral societies in Lancashire and Yorkshire in the 19th century, yet in the 20th century they are taken seriously only by the long hair and sandals brigade, who fortunately, are keeping them alive and perhaps one day they'll emerge like butterflies to amaze and amuse us all again with their contrapuntal part writing and hidden witticisms.

In the 1920s and 30s the chorus travelled to massed rehearsals and away Festivals by train, all crowding onto the same one and keeping seats for their friends. The railway companies would have had prior warning of the Festival and made special arrangements for visitors coming from London, Birmingham and Bristol. There are stories in the family archive of a Worcester year when the engine pulling the train in which the Hereford contingent of the chorus were coming back from a massed rehearsal, had problems with the gradient through the tunnel under the Malverns and finally broke down at Colwall before attempting the second tunnel. Taxis were sent to convey the ladies to Ledbury, but the men had to walk. Eventually a spare train arrived from Hereford and everybody arrived home four hours later, at midnight!

The cost of living remained at a constant level in those days and lodgings at boarding houses and inns in Worcester were £1 15s per week. The chorus received £3 for their living expenses and had to buy their own copies of Messiah and Elijah. Men wore their best suits, which were always dark cloth, and the ladies covered their heads, not always with a hat as in pre-war times, but with a veil, 'like that of a novice in a convent' or as one lady remembers, 'a little piece of black lace, which we did clever things with.' This same lady was invited to join the Festival Class in 1939 with her sister and close friend, all of whom were already singing in a chamber choir run by one of the lay-clerks, a natural feeding ground for the chorus. According to her account, the numbers of singers wishing to join exceeded the requirements so when the Festival was away and only a very few were needed, they would share a seat on the platform, one singing one night and the other the next.

Some remnants of the 18th and 19th century traditions remained. Chorus and orchestra were still entertained to a breakfast by the stewards or the Dean, a custom dating back to the time when Ellen, Sarah, Mr. Giardini and Mr. Malchair and their fellow performers were welcomed to the Meetings by the two stewards who gave generously toward the expenses of the week. In the 1920s, many of the same families of landed gentry were still underwriting the Festival. Without the practical and financial help from these people, for whom it was still a major event in the social calendar, besides a musical one, it may not have survived the years of strikes and depression.

The 20 years between the world wars saw more new names in the programmes. English choral music had ripened into a harvest at last. Ethel Smythe's Mass at Gloucester in 1925 and Canticle of Spring the following year at Worcester, Vaughan Williams' Sancta Civitas at Worcester in 1929, Delius' Song before Sunrise at Hereford in 1930, Holst's Hymn of Jesus and Choral Fantasia at Gloucester in 1931, Vaughan Williams' Benedicite and Magnificat at Worcester the following year, George Dyson's St. Paul's Voyage to Melita and Bliss' Morning Heroes at Hereford in 1933, along with Vaughan Williams' Six Choral Songs and his Dona Nobis Pacem at Gloucester in 1937. Add to these a kaleidoscope of works by European composers—Rossini's Stabat Mater at Hereford in 1924, Kodaly's Psalmus Hungaricus at Gloucester in 1928 and Budavari Te Deum, also at Gloucester but in 1937, Honegger's King David at Gloucester in 1928, the late arrival of Bach's St. John Passion in Worcester in 1929, Szymanowsky's Stabat Mater at Worcester in 1932, and Fauré's Requiem at Worcester in 1938, and the spectrum is seen to be broadening considerably, giving the chorus some very interesting rehearsal times. Audiences continued to flock, the list of subscribers was long, in 1925 the festival went on air, and although 1934 was a year of mourning for Elgar, Delius and Holst, their music was firmly rooted in the Three Choirs repertoire.

Again, as if the first time wasn't bad enough, the love of power supplanted the power of love and war broke out just as final rehearsals for the 1939 Festival in Hereford were taking place. Large public meetings were prohibited so there was no alternative but to cancel.

The programme had been planned as follows:-

SEPT. 3.	SUNDAY.		**In the Cathedral**
2.45.	Opening Service.		
SEPT. 5.	TUESDAY.		
11.15.	" The Kingdom "		*Elgar*
2.30.	" Elegy " for Soloists, Chorus and Orchestra		
	(First Performance) ...		*Brent Smith*
	" O amantissime sponse Jesu " ...		*Ritter*
	Symphony in G minor ...		*Mozart*
7.30.	" Elijah "		*Mendelssohn*
SEPT. 6.	WEDNESDAY.		
11.15.	" Mass in B Minor "		*Bach*
2.30.	" Mass in B Minor " (concluded)		
	" Pastoral " Symphony ... *Vaughan Williams*		
SEPT. 7.	THURSDAY.		
11.15.	Variations for Orchestra (on the Chorale		
	" St. Antoni ") ... ... *Brahms*		
	" Quo Vadis " for Soloists, Chorus and		
	Orchestra (First Performance) ...		
			George Dyson
2.30.	" Job " (Scenes 3 and 4)		*Parry*
	Five Variants of " Dives and Lazarus "		
	(*First performance in England*) *Vaughan Williams*		
	" Dona Nobis Pacem " ... *Vaughan Williams*		
7.30.	" The Dream of Gerontius " ...		*Elgar*
SEPT. 8.	FRIDAY.		
11.15.	" The Creation " (Part I.)		*Haydn*
	" Dies Natalis," for Soprano Solo and		
	Strings (First Performance)		
			Gerald Finzi
	Violin Concerto in G		*Mozart*
2.30.	" The Messiah " (Selection)... ...		*Handel*

There was to have been an opening service of great splendour and three very full days. All this is printed on a small card, the size of a postcard, a far cry from the glossy, computer generated brochure of today. Once again the ideas were shelved, the Festival was sent off to its air-raid shelter for seven years and the disappointments were great. Among the chorus were some who would have been singing for the first time, for whom it had been a childhood ambition as they watched the triennial gathering and procession into the cathedral of smartly dressed audience and black-clothed performers. Morning, afternoon and evening, they, on the outside, could hear music coming from inside, with no hope of getting any closer. Not for the likes of ordinary folk unless they could sing and join the chorus.

14 On Wings of Song

Such harmony is in immortal souls.
From 'The Merchant of Venice', by William Shakespeare

After six years of musical deprivation, it was Hereford's responsibility to take the Festival out of hiding and prove to the world that, though threatened, it cannot be stopped. Young men and women back from the army, farmwork, munitions' factories or nursing, sought some means of righting the balance of life.

The three cathedral organists, Hull, Atkins and Sumsion and their musicians were faced with real belt-tightening austerity. The days of lavish and leisured entertainment were gone for ever. Clothing coupons and ration books dominated people's lives, deciding what they could eat and how they should dress, but at least the black-out had come down and the gas-masks and identity cards had gone to the museum. By some miracle the organisers of these post-war years managed to feed and water orchestras, chorus, soloists and visitors and the delight of reunion must have helped to push officialdom and bureaucracy into the background.

Through all these struggles there came new music in abundance. Kodaly already had a strong link with the Three Choirs and conducted his Missa Brevis in 1948 (W), whilst Gerald Finzi's Intimations of Immortality in 1950 (G) brought serenity, grace and vitality all rolled into one. In that same year the new harmonic style of Howells' Hymnus Paradisi demanded a musically literate chorus and some had to drop out. Berlioz's Childhood of Christ was performed in Hereford in 1952.

By this time David Willcocks was organist at Worcester and Meredith Davies at Hereford, two young men who knew that the Meetings of the Three

Choirs had to move with the times as far as standard of performance was concerned, or sink into oblivion as 'an old-fashioned amateur junketing'— fighting talk from some of the critics! There was a desperate need for improvement in the rehearsal conditions for chorus and orchestra. Without some extra time allotted to the final rehearsals there was no hope. In 1953 for instance, everything was supposed to be perfected in $2^{1}/_{2}$ hours on Saturday and $2^{1}/_{2}$ hours on Monday. The management was *not* moving with the times at all. Elijah had 45 minutes, the St. John Passion 30 minutes, Walton's Te Deum, a new piece, 30 minutes, Israel in Egypt 40 minutes and Monteverdi's Magnificat, receiving its first performance at the Three Choirs, 30 minutes, and of those, only 15 with orchestra. This is quite horrifying for those who know the length and complexities of these works, and remembering that the presence of the orchestra is not always immediately helpful as far as finding the notes is concerned. Five years later, midst a very full programme at Hereford, Monteverdi's Vespers of the Blessed Virgin (1610) were given their first performance at the Festival. Is it possible to imagine the effect of this vast contrapuntal work on singers brought up on Elijah and Messiah? Some members of that chorus still tell tales of how they were completely lost through inadequate preparation. Messrs. Davies, Willcocks and Sumsion attacked the problem of meagre rehearsal time with gusto and managed to gather orchestra and chorus together for an extra session. But this didn't come about without heart searching and pocket emptying.

The chorus still sat on planks of wood with nothing to lean against except the knees of the one behind, and lucky if they weren't knobbly. Reading from single part copies with little indication of where to come in, other than a tune for the celeste which couldn't be heard because it was behind a pillar, they developed a skill for picking notes from thin air. But gradually the schedule did get better, more attuned to the demands of the 20th century and its monotonal, bitonal and atonal music.

Varying time signatures presented new problems. Most of us can count in 3/4 or 4/4 time, but five or seven beats in a bar makes one pause for thought and there is no time for that. Stravinsky's Symphony of Psalms, performed in 1955 at Hereford, is extravagant with changes of time signature and syncopation—another interesting diversion, for which not all have a natural gift. This felled a few more followers from the back rows of the chorus ready for 1957 at Worcester, when, like a firework bursting a cascade of light over the Festival scene, there came Belshazzar's Feast. William Walton's writing has a

THE THREE CHOIRS FESTIVAL
1957

WORCESTER
MUSIC MEETING

Monday Evening
September 2nd, at 7.0
In the Cathedral

SACRED SERVICE—*Ernest Bloch*

INTRODUCTION AND ALLEGRO
—*Elgar*

BELSHAZZAR'S FEAST
—*William Walton*

THE CITY OF BIRMINGHAM SYMPHONY ORCHESTRA
(Leader: NORRIS STANLEY)

Conducted by DAVID WILLCOCKS

ANNOTATED WORD BOOK
(*copyright*)
Price One Shilling and Sixpence

Front of the programme for 2nd September 1957

directness which leaves no doubt as to the desired effect. Belshazzar is definitely one of the pinnacles to which we aspire, and having reached can follow with Britten's War Requiem in 1963 (W) and Tippett's Child of our Time in 1966 (W).

The Audition

Barely five minutes in the company of the chorus master can reduce a normally well balanced human to a shaking jelly. Fear of looking foolish is uppermost; fright closes the throat and a strangled croak leaves its perpetrator wishing the floor would open up; terror wipes out all previous knowledge of perfect fifths and dominant sevenths, and a fairly ordinary piece of sight-reading brings on dyslexia in a big way. Nevertheless, application forms are filled in, voices are heard and in the fullness of time the required number of singers receive the following communication:

> Dear ......,
> You are invited to sing at this year's Three Choirs Festival.
> I enclose a list of rehearsal dates. You are expected to attend at least 75%. and I would be grateful if you would let me know if you are unavoidably prevented from doing this.
> Private practice on scores is essential.
> You are reminded to sign the register on arrival and always bring a pencil.
>
> Chorus Superintendent.

Unfortunately, not everybody has the right tone of voice, and others find an unsurmountable problem in sight-reading a four-part fugue. Failing an audition can be devastating. There was one dear lady to whom the music meant everything, who worked her way through Beethoven's Piano Sonatas and struggled with Grade V Theory, but on being omitted from the chorus list could not face the world and chose to end her life with an overdose of sleeping pills. It is impossible to over-estimate the depth of despair felt by those whose need for music goes unnourished.

Every year young singers are welcomed into the chorus for the first time.

15 Hallelujah

O Sing unto the Lord a new Song.

Prayer Book, 1662

March

Dear Gran,
Thanks a lot for your copy of the Verdi. We've already started rehearsals. Steve and I are first basses. The other two are as old as grandad. Some of the ladies must be nearly ninety but they can still sing. The sound is terrific, especially when we do the Requiem. That Dies Irae is fantastic! One of the altos remembers Uncle Donald.
Love,
John

April

My dear John,
I am so glad you are enjoying Festival Class - as we used to call it. I laughed at your description of the elderly ladies, because I remember having the same impression when I first joined at the age of twenty, like you. I don't expect they are so terribly old really, and anyway, singing keeps the body young and the mind alert.
Donald came round last night and we had a good evening remembering some wonderful concerts and the high jinks off the platform.

He remembers the first time that there was clapping at the end of a cathedral concert. This was in 1969 after Christopher Robinson conducted a very difficult new work by Jonathan Harvey, called Ludus Amoris. Nothing like this had ever been sung by the Three Choirs and neither had the audience applauded. After all, this was a church and a certain sort of restrained behaviour is expected. Nowadays you'll probably find that everything is applauded unless the Dean specially asks for a more reverent reception. I too remember this piece. We could not make head nor tail of it when we first saw the score, though it did get quite exciting as time went on. The three organists at the time, Robinson, Lloyd and Sanders were very patient and persevering, but the work was a shock to the Three Choirs system. Spoken whisperings rising to hysterical crescendos, cocktail party conversations and a simulated Trafalgar Square demonstration against war were not regular Festival fare and we found it embarrassing to have to shout in the cathedral. Our reper-toire had widened since the days of The Messiah, Elijah and The Dream of Gerontius, and even some of the audience wondered. Nevertheless the Royal Philharmonic Orchestra, who played at the first performance in Worcester, thought it should be repeated and most of the chorus travelled to London's Festival Hall to try it again; not with great success it has to be said. In fact, without the cathe-dral's masking acoustic the mistakes and uncertainties showed up even more. The small audience clapped politely and went home and the chorus got back on their buses with a feeling of anti-climax. We felt slightly irritated at having been presented with notation more suited to the style and capabilities of a professional choir; and sympathy for the composer who had something important to say but whom we had failed. Yet this was to be but a forerunner of future 'protest' pieces.

Will you be staying over for the Festival? I remember that the visiting contingents used to stay at the College of Education along with half the audience and the whole of the orchestra, and that was quite a party. In those days we had V.I.P. treatment. Morning coffee and afternoon tea were served as well as all the other meals

Richard Lloyd rehearsing in 1973

although there never was time to eat them all. I hear they don't provide food now so your mother will have to send you off with a food parcel. A week away from home can be very expensive these days if you are not careful. The washing facilities at the college were a bit sparse but I don't suppose that would worry you!

Good luck with the new piece. Let me know how rehearsals go.

Much love,

Gran

May

Dear Gran

Just a quick line as I'm due out in ten minutes.

We had the first Massed Rehearsal last night and I have to tell you about that to see if it was the same as in your day. We were in the Chapter House, and just being in that building made me want to sing. The sound of the full chorus is just HUGE. There are 190 of us and I've never felt or heard anything like this in my whole life. The conductor made us sing pianissimo too and that was just magical. The new piece is going to be O.K. How is your Russian? I'll come round next week and show why I ask.

Love,
John.

May

My dear John,

How nice to meet Sally. I thought you said all the Sopranos were nearly ninety! You both seem to be enjoying rehearsals. Thank you both for the impromptu recital of music from the programme, especially the Russian work. Sally has a lovely voice. She tells me she is going to Music College in London next term. I wish her well.

Hearing you two discuss the problems with reading Russian reminded me of the Glagolitic Mass by Janacek in Czech, Bernstein's Chichester Psalms and Bloch's Sacred Service in Hebrew, Orff's Carmina Burana in old Latin, Berlioz's L'enfance du Christ in French, the Mahler symphonies in German, Prokofiev's Alexander Nevsky in Russian, and much more.

Unfortunately, we didn't always know what we were singing about because there was no translation, and that was a big hindrance in performance. The words are so important to the meaning of the music and I remember with gratitude one particular conductor who took time to explain the passion needed for the few bars sung in German at the end of a Mahler Symphony, and again in Act I of Wagner's Parsifal. It made all the difference to our understanding of the music. None of us enjoyed simply mouthing the words like puppets.

We do expect a great deal from our cathedral organists. To be in charge of the Three Choirs Festival nowadays is not just a job for a master of organ technique and choir training, but for a linguist, an orchestral conductor and a diplomat. Those of recent years, Cook,

Willcocks, Davies, Lloyd, Sanders, Guest, Robinson, Massey, Hunt, Briggs and Lucas, have triumphed over many adversities and we in the chorus have watched their struggles. We know that the Festival makes enormous demands on them and have always done our best to help - particularly when they have remembered to smile at us!

1969 may well be remembered for its innovative programme. We felt safer with Britten's Spring Symphony the next year, although this too had tricky moments and there was even less room to sit, stand and breathe when the choristers were with us on the platform. I remember one little boy called Robert, who couldn't have been more than eight years old. His eyes were like saucers as he watched the orchestra. What an experience for this youngster. I wonder what he remembers now from a 'boneless, quaking fish, eating for cold his aching feet;' I think it would have given me nightmares, but maybe little boys are tough. They certainly enjoyed singing this:

When as the rye reach to the chin,
And chopcherry, chopcherry ripe within,
Strawberries swimming in the cream,
And school boys playing in the stream;

Love,
Gran

June

Dear Gran,
Not many more weeks to go before the Festival. There is a bit of a crisis as the new piece hasn't arrived from the composer.

Love,
John

June

My dear John,
So you still await the new piece. There have been other emergencies over lost or late scores. I remember one traumatic non-arrival in 1977. This year was nominally the 250th Three Choirs Festival and also the Queen's Silver Jubilee. For this The Master of the Queen's Musik had written 'A Mass for Christ the King'. Unfortunately, the pressure of completion date had a dessicating effect on inspiration and we all felt for Malcolm Williamson as he struggled to deliver on time, desperately handing page after page of manuscript to the conductor on the very morning of performance. In the event we performed as much as we could of this devoutly inspired work and on its completion the following year, were invited to give a full performance in Westminster Cathedral in which we were joined by the Goldsmith's Choral Union, conducted by Sir Charles Groves in the presence of the Queen Mother, and all went well.

I remember well the excitement at the arrival of a commissioned work; and the despair, bewilderment or delight engendered by the first run through. Sometimes the composer would sit in on a rehearsal and I always used to wonder how he or she could cope with sounds so far removed from those heard in the imagination.

Usually after the performance, the composer came to the front to acknowledge the ovation. Occasionally, in more recent years we watched casually dressed and ill-at-ease composers shuffle onto the platform looking self conscious amongst the orchestral players in their immaculate evening dress. Coloured shirts and corduroy trousers were not the order of the day when I was a young girl, but fashions in dress and behaviour have changed beyond recognition since then.

I do hope your new piece arrives in time and that it is printed clearly.

Your loving Gran.

July

Dear Gran,

We have now had combined rehearsals with all three conductors. They tell jokes and time goes fast. I could do with twice as much rehearsal time because all this is new to me. Some people have sung everything except the new piece many times over and can go right through the Verdi Requiem without looking at the copy! I shall be able to do that next time.

Look out for me on the platform.

Love,
John

July

My dear John,

I enjoyed reading about the jokes at rehearsal. It always helps if conductors are in a good mood, though I suppose we should sympathise with them when they are anxious about things not going well. There are still a few of the old school who think sarcasm is the only way to get results from a bunch of amateur singers. It doesn't work. Feelings are hurt, people become rebellious and the spirit of the music suffers. Do you remember reading about the mill-workers in the north of England who were prepared to trudge twenty miles to choir practice? We may not have to trudge nowadays but we are still as dedicated and a bit of encouragement from the front makes all the difference to our confidence.

Let me have your rehearsal schedule for the week so that I can come to some of the sessions. You'll have a shock when the orchestra is on the platform with you. Each year there seem to be more of them, and they are always very loud.

Love,
Gran

August

Dear Gran,
Here is the schedule and two tickets for the Opening Service.

Love,
John

August

Dear John,
I have enjoyed your letters so much. They have made me re-live my years of choral singing; and I know you must be very excited. Has anyone warned you that it will be very hot on the platform?

Long ago, the Festival was held in September to suit the end of harvest and the diaries of the county socialites, but when new music became more complex and in need of thorough rehearsals with orchestra, the chorus found themselves having to ask for a week away from work in order to fulfil their commitments. Many took their annual leave in Festival week, but this was not possible for the many teachers in the ranks, and others felt it would be wise to move the Festival into August when holidays were in mind. As August weather can be hot and thundery, concert dress gradually became minimal in weight, until the long hot summer of 1976 peaked at tropical temperatures and the gentlemen were allowed to remove their jackets and appear in shirt sleeve order. Thus was another convention shattered. Ladies were no longer required to cover their heads in church but even so there was great discomfort on the platform with a large choir of 270 wedged so tightly that we were almost welded together and forced to move en bloc. To add to the discomfort of natural summer heat, during the 1970s closed circuit television was installed for the benefit of listeners sitting out of sight, as many have to in a building of giant pillars. For the CCTV to be effective, extra lighting was installed and the chorus found out what it felt like to be set on high in an incubator set on High.

The Festival Chorus conducted by Roy Massey in 1991

One year we had to sing through a tremendous thunderstorm that accompanied a performance of *Caractacus* which we were performing in a Leisure Centre. The story of the Roman invasion of the Malverns probably wasn't thought suitable for the cathedral, but as an Elgar work, it had to be performed somewhere - even in this bizarre building. The impact of hailstones on the tin roof added something to Elgar's orchestration which he hadn't intended but would have found amusing, I'm sure, since he was a man of jokes and japes.

Another expedition to a Leisure Centre was in 1980 for the *African Sanctus* by David Fanshawe. At the end of a tremendously exhilarating concert the appearance of the composer throwing flowers to the choir only added to the theatricality of the music. Singing in tandem with tapes of African singers and drummers was another first for a chorus fed on liturgical text. I can't imagine how my grandfather would have reacted to this, but we found it a very moving experience. Would that they had let us dance too!

And now it is your turn.

I know you will enjoy the week, and probably come away from it completely dazed and exhausted, but every moment will stay with you for the rest of your life and shape your future as it has mine and countless others over three centuries.

Much love,

Gran.

P.S.

I shall be so proud to see you up there on the platform at the Opening Service.

O may we soon again renew that song,
And keep in tune with Heaven, till God ere long
To his celestial concert us unite,
To live with him, and sing in endless morns of light.

Ode 'At a Solemn Music' by Milton/Parry

'... and tho' the Members, being voluntary, may go off as their wills vary, or as their affairs require, yet, by the succession of others the Society may subsist for many Years, yea, generations; which tends to the furtherance of God's glory in the exaltation of his holy worship, to the improvement of our Choirs, the credit of our Foundations, to the benefit of our Cities, the comfort of the fatherless, to the delight of mankind, of ourselves, and all that come nigh us. Upon these grounds it commenced, and upon these let our brotherly love continue.'

Sermon preached by Thomas Bisse, Chancellor of Hereford
3rd September, 1729

Bibliography

Boden, Anthony *Three Choirs. A History of the Festival* Alan Sutton, 1992

Burney, Dr. Charles *A History of Music* 1789

Cunliffe, Barry *History of Bath Alan* Sutton

Edwards, R.A. *And the Glory,* Maney & son, 1985

Firth *Bradford and the Industrial Revolution* 1990

Fraser (ed.) *A History of Modern Leeds* 1980

Gardiner, John *Music and Friends* 1830

Grove *History of Music*

Herbage, Julian *Messiah* 1948

Hunt, Donald *Festival Memorie*s 1996

Lysons & Amott, Williams & Chance *Annals of the Three Choirs* Chance, 1895

Mackerness *Social History of English Music* Routledge and Kegan Paul, 1964

Mrs. Jordan's Profession

North, Roger *Memoirs of Music* 1728

Parsons, Mary *A Prevailing Passion (Worcester)* 1996

Russell, David *Popular Music in England* MUP, 1987

Scholes *The Oxford Companion to Music* O.U.P., 1970

Sewell, G.F. *Bradford Festival Choral Society* Bradford, 1907

Shaw, Watkins *The Three Choirs Festival* Baylis & Son 1954

Thomas, Aneurin *Con Molto Piacere (Hereford)* 1987

Tilliard, Stella *Citizen Lord* Chatto and Windus

Young, Percy *The Choral Tradition* Hutchinson 1962

References

Chapter 3
1. Shaw Church Records.
2. T.S. Eliot said much later in his *Notes towards the Definition of Culture* (1948).

Chapter 4
1. Roger North, *Memoirs of Music*, 1728.

Chapter 7
1. Except where otherwise stated, he accounts of visiting singers are largely to be found in the *Annals of the Three Choirs*, Lysons & Amott, Williams & Chance.
2. Genealogical Memorials of the Travis Family, J. Travis, Walsden, 1893
3. *The Three Choirs Festival*, Watkins Shaw.
4. Ibid.
5. Ibid.

Chapter 10
1. Except where otherwise stated, he accounts of visiting singers are largely to be found in the *Annals of the Three Choirs*, by Lysons & Amott, Williams & Chance.
2. *A History of Bradford Festival Choral Society*, by G.F. Sewell, 1907
3. Ibid.
4. Ibid.